New Monologues for Women

New Monologues for Women

Edited by
GEOFFREY COLMAN

methuen | drama

LONDON • NEW YORK • OXFORD • NEW DELHI • SYDNEY

METHUEN DRAMA
Bloomsbury Publishing Plc
50 Bedford Square, London, WC1B 3DP, UK
1385 Broadway, New York, NY 10018, USA
29 Earlsfort Terrace, Dublin 2, Ireland

BLOOMSBURY, METHUEN DRAMA and the Methuen Drama logo are
trademarks of Bloomsbury Publishing Plc

First published 2016
Reprinted 2016, 2017, 2019, 2020, 2021, 2022, 2023, 2024

Editorial notes © Geoffrey Colman, 2016

Cover design: Jesse Holborn

A catalogue record for this book is available from the British Library.

A catalog record for this book is available from the Library of Congress.

ISBN: PB: 978-1-4725-7351-3
ePDF: 978-1-4725-7353-7
eBook: 978-1-4725-7354-4

Typeset by Fakenham Prepress Solutions, Fakenham, Norfolk NR21 8NN
Printed and bound in Great Britain

To find out more about our authors and books visit www.bloomsbury.com
and sign up for our newsletters.

Contents

Performing Rights

Best Man by Carmel Winters
The Agency (London) Ltd, 24 Pottery Lane, London W11 4LZ, www.theagency.co.uk

Birthday by Joe Penhall
Judy Daish Associates Limited, 2 St Charles Place, London W10 6EG

Black Jesus by Anders Lustgarten
Curtis Brown Group Limited, Haymarket House, 28–29 Haymarket, London SW1Y 4SP

Brief Encounter adapted by Emma Rice
Alan Brodie Representation Ltd, www.alanbrodie.com, abr@alanbrodie.com

Can't Forget About You by David Ireland
Alan Brodie Representation Ltd, www.alanbrodie.com, abr@alanbrodie.com

Candide by Mark Ravenhill
Casarotto Ramsay & Associates Ltd, Waverley House, 7–12 Noel Street, London W1F 8GQ, rights@casarotto.co.uk

Cannibals by Rory Mullarkey
Casarotto Ramsay & Associates Ltd, Waverley House, 7–12 Noel Street, London W1F 8GQ, rights@casarotto.co.uk

Casualties by Ross Ericson
By professionals to Grist To The Mill Productions Ltd (info@gristtheatre.co.uk) and by amateurs to Permissions Department, Methuen Drama, Bloomsbury Publishing Plc, 50 Bedford Square, London WC1B 3DP (performance.permissions@bloomsbury.com)

City Love by Simon Vinnicombe
The Agency (London) Ltd, 24 Pottery Lane, London W11 4LZ, www.theagency.co.uk

Clean by Sabrina Mahfouz
Curtis Brown Group Limited, Haymarket House, 28–29 Haymarket, London SW1Y 4SP

The Curious Incident of the Dog in the Night-Time adapted by Simon Stephens
Casarotto Ramsay & Associates Ltd, Waverley House, 7–12 Noel Street, London W1F 8GQ, rights@casarotto.co.uk

Dark Vanilla Jungle by Philip Ridley
Knight Hall Agency Limited, Lower Ground Floor, 7 Mallow Street, London EC1Y 8RQ

Dirty Great Love Story by Richard Marsh and Katie Bonna
United Agents, 12–26 Lexington Street, London W1F 0LE

A Doll's House adapted by Simon Stephens
Casarotto Ramsay & Associates Ltd, Waverley House, 7–12 Noel Street, London W1F 8GQ, rights@casarotto.co.uk

Dry Ice by Sabrina Mahfouz
Curtis Brown Group Limited, Haymarket House, 28–29 Haymarket, London SW1Y 4SP

The Effect by Lucy Prebble
Knight Hall Agency Limited, Lower Ground Floor, 7 Mallow Street, London EC1Y 8RQ

Exit by Steven Berkoff
Rosica Colin Limited, 1 Clareville Grove Mews, London SW7 5AH

Free Fall by Vinay Patel
Sayle Screen Limited, 11 Jubilee Place, London SW3 3TD

Hidden in the Sand by James Phillips
Independent Talent Group Ltd, 40 Whitfield Street, London W1T 2RH

A History of Falling Things by James Graham
By professionals to Curtis Brown Group Limited, Haymarket House, 28–29 Haymarket, London SW1Y 4SP and by amateurs to Permissions Department, Methuen Drama, Bloomsbury Publishing Plc, 50 Bedford Square, London WC1B 3DP, performance.permissions@bloomsbury.com

If You Don't Let Us Dream, We Won't Let You Sleep by Anders Lustgarten
Curtis Brown Group Limited, Haymarket House, 28–29 Haymarket, London SW1Y 4SP

Josephine and I by Cush Jumbo
Curtis Brown Group Limited, Haymarket House, 28–29 Haymarket, London SW1Y 4SP

The Kindness of Strangers by Curious Directive
Curious Directive, info@curiousdirective.com

McQueen, or Lee and Beauty by James Phillips
Independent Talent Group Ltd, 40 Whitfield Street, London W1T 2RH

Morning by Simon Stephens
Casarotto Ramsay & Associates Ltd, Waverley House, 7–12 Noel Street, London W1F 8GQ, rights@casarotto.co.uk

Playing With Grown-ups by Hannah Patterson
By professionals to Curtis Brown Group Limited, Haymarket House, 28–29 Haymarket, London SW1Y 4SP and by amateurs to Permissions Department, Methuen Drama, Bloomsbury Publishing Plc, 50 Bedford Square, London WC1B 3DP, performance.permissions@bloomsbury.com

Quiz Show by Rob Drummond
Casarotto Ramsay & Associates Ltd, Waverley House, 7–12 Noel Street, London W1F 8GQ, rights@casarotto.co.uk

Red Velvet by Lolita Chakrabarti
The Agency (London) Ltd, 24 Pottery Lane, London W11 4LZ, www.theagency.co.uk

Skin Tight by Gary Henderson
Playmarket, New Zealand, agency@playmarket.org.nz

Underneath by Pat Kinevane
Fishamble, Shamrock Chambers, 1/2 Eustace Street, Dublin 2, Ireland

Wasted by Kate Tempest
Fox Mason Ltd, 36–38 Glasshouse St, London W1B 5DL

The Wolf from the Door by Rory Mullarkey
Casarotto Ramsay & Associates Ltd, Waverley House, 7–12 Noel Street, London W1F 8GQ, rights@casarotto.co.uk

You're Not Like The Other Girls Chrissy by Caroline Horton
Curtis Brown Group Limited, Haymarket House, 28–29 Haymarket, London SW1Y 4SP

Introduction

The choice of speech can overly preoccupy even the most experienced actor when asked to present one for audition. Many work hard to unearth ever more obscure or astounding extracts, as if freakishness will give edge or value. However such effort reveals nothing of actual use or benefit. A speech should be selected only if it enables a simple, clear route into the actor's imaginative realm. It should enable the useful demonstration of both creative and technical abilities and allow the actor to enter its imaginary world without a fight. Equally – from my own perspective as a director, coach and acting teacher – I have found that actors should generally avoid 'putting on' voices and much worked upon accents unless specifically required, for they always tend to upstage both actor and speech. Avoidance should also be the key rule where props are concerned.

Each speech in this collection is set in its performance context and accompanied by notes intended to open up possibilities for the actor, encouraging them to ask questions and to make informed and imaginative decisions about their character and their performance. My interest here is not literary criticism but rather how a piece of theatre gets into the space. This book is not, therefore, an instruction manual, but a series of markers on a creative map that doesn't really exist until you, the actor, start to put down the coordinates.

It is a rare thing indeed to be asked to audition in silence, whatever the context. In our own lives we negotiate the very act of 'being', thinking through both silence and also crucially through language – the absence of silence. Ideally, the audition process would embrace both aspects of this personal and public negotiation, but more typically (in the early stages, at least) it focuses on the immediate 'close up' of the spoken moment. The monologue is the necessary bit of the deal – the bit that actors have to get right, often in the space of 120 seconds. As an isolated piece of text, the audition speech could be seen as nothing more than a functional cultural phenomenon – an oddity or transaction solely created for a synthetic awkward moment.

Books containing audition monologues will have necessarily been through the rather sordid editorial process of cutting speeches out of existing plays, unless they have been especially written, like the grandiose patter of the old vaudevillian[1] turn. Cutting the spoken word – from the

---

[1] The vaudevillian monologist was a prized and popular entertainer in the theatres of the late nineteenth and early twentieth centuries where Music Hall and Variety entertainment craved both the salacious and the sentimental. The tradition went into decline after the First World War and subsequent rise of cinema.

moment it was necessary to speak it – is fraught with problems both editorially and theatrically. In the wrong hands, thoughts selected and edited form their cast iron emotional narratives and clear beginning, middle and end can remain like stolen, potentially useless limbs separated from a whole dramatic body. For the actor, the skill required when preparing a monologue for audition or performance is to bring the whole body back to life with the use of just one limb. Such a task is complex and virtually impossible in that an entire play cannot be assumed into the space of the two mythical minutes of an audition speech – nor should it be. A new world will need to be created: a world that breathes the memory and same oxygen of its former completeness, but a world that will necessarily be autonomous in shape and form.

It might be useful at this point to clarify what is actually meant by the terms 'monologue', 'soliloquy' and 'speech', for they are so interchangeably used that their resulting definitions are promiscuously vague and unhelpful. Of course in general terms, a speech is in some ways formal, in that it is usually delivered to a group of people or audience. It is not usually connected to, or part of anything else. The Political speech, Queen's speech, or even Best Man's speech exists outside of the more usual utterances of the politician, monarch or nervous best man, because these are constructed. As a literary term, 'monologue' has been so variously appropriated that – outside of academic study – it has come to mean all things and nothing. Simply put, a monologue is an extended set of spoken thoughts, ideas or reflections. Sometimes also called an 'interior monologue', it is uttered from the more usual interior world of hidden thought and is therefore uniquely experienced in performance by the world that has the rare privilege to hear it. In contrast, a 'dramatic monologue'[2] is not explicitly concerned with the hidden or interior moments of being, but is where a character speaks to another character. Hidden thoughts may be revealed, but they are offered as opposed to witnessed. Of course countless other labels abound, but they are more concerned with literary criticism and function and not the performance moment. But of the multitude, the label 'narrative monologue' should also be noted here. This is where a character quite literally tells a story, usually about something that has happened in the past. The Elizabethan or Jacobean monologue is more typically and correctly described as 'soliloquy' – that is when a character speaks the very private world of their thoughts as only witnessed by the audience or camera. (*'To be or not to be'* etc.) Again, all are essentially the same, but the correct

---

[2] Robert Browning's 'My Last Duchess' (1842) is a very good example of the dramatic monologue.

identification of the type of speech may usefully offer the actor some essential clues into the dramatic sense of the performance moment. As in life, hidden thoughts are often very different to shared thoughts.

When confronted by the excitement and possibility of so many speeches, I imagine a sort of 'extract vertigo' may gradually overwhelm even the sturdiest of performers. So many choices will not necessarily give the much hoped for instant or direct hit – a eureka moment where all aspects of craft and ambition are usefully located in just nineteen lines. Speeches may blur and congeal into a mass of words short circuiting the hunt and rendering a form of performance blindness which can be very dispiriting. But to put this into context, if this book were a compilation album of last year's greatest hits, it would be very unusual for the listener to celebrate and adore each and every piece of music with the same passion or interest. A silent filter in our heads sifts music into various emotional stacks, graded by the nearness or distance to one's own taste. Similarly, therefore, it would be unimaginably strange if each speech published here is the best one you have ever read or the one that you simply must perform. There will of course be some that will not even be read to completion and others that will be dwelt upon and cherished for years to come. Selection is primarily driven by personal preference, but it may have to be governed by particular professional requirements as stated by those holding the audition or workshop – requirements such as period, genre, performance style, language, accent, status, role, etc. The list could go on.

To select and perform a solo speech is not only to offer an immediate characterful outpouring, but to also convey technical ability, craft and skill. The monologue is not a time to demonstrate what might be: it should demonstrate what is. There may well be an ageing King Lear or Lady Macbeth in the furthest point of your career, but the director, acting coach or audition panellist will require you to be very much in the present. A speech is not in that sense a future forecast but an accurate measure of the possibility of 'now'. Selection should be about finding words and ideas that create the enabling conditions for you to show the best of your creative response to character.

In a recent conversation with playwright Simon Stevens, I asked him if, when writing, he saw the actual physical worlds of his plays: the sky, the rooms and buildings of the incredible, beautiful, dangerous places that he imagines. His answer was striking in that, for a writer of such vivid sensual and emotional skill, he said that what he actually saw was 'just the theatre,' just the machine itself: a black floor, walls, lights and rows where the audience sit. His theatre is thus a provocation for both actor and audience member to place imagination at the centre of the creative moment. As you read through these speeches you may have to make a similar decision: The machine or the physical world? You will need to be vigilant and carefully analyse any implied dramatic conventions as demonstrated through the use of stage space. The fictional 'real world' space with its sky, grass, towering building or battlefields is also very dependent on the actor's understanding of the social and cultural meaning of the world that will be inhabited. The necessity for the actor to identify spatial and aesthetic context is discussed in much of Stanislavki's famous writings, where the character's world is utterly dependent on the Given Circumstances. The challenge is quite an extraordinary one: to bring to life the physical and emotional world of a play – the union of creative and technical skill – performed in seconds.

The successful realisation of a 'truthful' audition seems to be increasingly only attainable through the successful performance of what could be described as a generalist or tele-visual performance style. Or, to put it another way, 'camera-real' acting: the acting that we see on our TV screens every day. Somehow, because it is the style we are most exposed to, it equates to a notion of good acting, and therefore by default, non-camera-real or abstract acting styles not seen on television equate to that of bad acting. When selecting possible speeches from this volume I would really urge you to consider that not all of them can be – or even should be – performed in the same way. How can they be performed irrespective of style or period? These speeches will require a sort of performance alertness if they are to be 'real'.

Geoffrey Colman

Best Man by Carmel Winters

*Don't think for one minute that I'm going to just disappear and let
the two of you play happy families ... That's not the deal here, that
is So not the deal.*

Best Man premiered at The Everyman, Cork, on 21 June 2013 as part of
Cork Midsummer Festival, and was directed by Michael Barker-Caven.

Context

High-flying real estate agent Kay Keane isn't just earning a living for
her family: she is making an absolute killing. Her stay-at-home husband,
having failed in his career, is looking after the children, but he would
rather be a novelist. Things are looking bad and the employment of a
helpful new nanny just makes matters worse. This comic, sometimes
grotesque, story about a modern family in crisis is brutal in its vision of
the domestic ideal.

Acting notes

In the first speech, Kay demonstrates to the new nanny, Marta, the all
the puffed-up, alpha-male punchiness of a real-estate trader in a Quentin
Tarantino movie. Selling, when ripping people off, is a 'fucking work
of art'. Kay intentionally uses the clichéd languages of a brutish floor-
trader, to show how successful she is. It's the 'pussies' that don't know
how to do their job. The real challenge will be to position this exterior
quality alongside her interior reasoning for doing so. Why would anyone
want to conduct themselves in this way? It is clear that Kay works in a
very competitive, male environment, and she seems to have lost sense of
who she really is. The performer must do the detective work to lift these
colossal slabs of put-on, learnt behaviour, and see what is underneath her
desire to be the 'best man'.

In the second speech, things have really collapsed. Kay and her husband
Alan find themselves in court, 'like a high-brow version of the Jerry
Springer Show'. Marta, the nanny who had been employed so that Alan
would have more time to write his best-selling novel, is now in a sexual
relationship with Kay. A story more incredible than anything he could
ever write. Kay once more demonstrates her need to be the 'best man'

by not only employing the attractive nanny, but also sleeping with her. Her actions have resulted in the custody of their child being fought over in court. Kay's behaviour is savaged by Alan, who finally finds purpose for his unused linguistic abilities by describing his wife's affair. Kay is spectacularly unrepentant about her actions and blocks out any glimmer of true reflection about what she has done to her marriage or her relationship with her child. Winters portrays a truly Machiavellian villain, one who would certainly be fun to explore in performance, but the delight of playing 'bad' could tip any portrayal into the pantomimic. Kay is not to be played for boos or hisses but, even in a sharp comedy such as this, must be given true psychological dimension. What drives her behaviour? What brings her happiness?

Irish

Kay   More than a sale, it was beautiful – it was a fucking work of art.
We had the asking in hand weeks ago – the vendor couldn't believe
his luck. Just short of a million for a white elephant he'd received in
lieu of a gambling debt of seventy grand a decade ago. Of course he
wanted to seize it immediately. Grab his loot and run. The other agents
were the same – there were three of us sharing the commission – the
other two pussies wanted to dash out and lodge the deposit and slap a
'Sale Agreed' on it quick before the buyer woke up and smelled his first
mortgage payment. But I had a hunch … The first client I'd shown it to
– a fat man with psoriasis and a greasy suit. He'd played his cards close
to his chest, scarcely looked at the'house. Just looked at the sitetwo
acres – asked about planning restrictions in the area, whether being a
period property there was a protection order on it.

'Wait,' I told the vendor, 'sit tight. It ain't over 'til the fat man sings
…'And he did. Just as the vendor was panicking our buyer would see
something decent and pull – in comes his bid, one point two million.
That's when the bottle of Bollinger was bought. I kept it corked, went
back to the first bidder. He was raging – not so much at the loss of the
house but that someone else had knocked him down a rung, climbed
ahead of him on the property ladder. That's when he started bidding with
his ego instead of his cheque book.

Irish

Kay   The judge is a woman. Early fifties, a mother, I guess, from the scuffed shoes, the ruined breasts …

Alan is thrilled. It's embarrassing, I imagine, with other men, admitting that the wife got the nanny … I've seen how other women's husbands look at me. Beyond the slur, beyond their giddy insecurity, it's there – a seam of pure admiration.

The judge draws her gown across her breasts and narrows her eyes at me as Alan recounts my crimes. I can hear how the writer in him corralled his words for the occasion. How he ransacked his thesaurus for multiple ways of calling me a drunken pervert. It's all laughably predictable. Like a high-brow version of the Jerry Springer Show except we're using two children and a jumble of legal jargon instead of fists.

I'm cold on the stand. I can see my solicitor looking worried. I'm not my own best witness. I'm looking at myself from somewhere very far away, hearing a voice trying to defend why it is I didn't make formal arrangements for access until now. Why I saw my children only three times in the month after I abandoned my family.

I am not very convincing, I have to admit. I hear the gap, the deficit. Three times in four weeks? Why did I let him prevent me? I can't speak. I'm trapped in Alan's parody of me … I imagine winking at the judge, slapping my thigh – telling her I had a very bad case of bed head that first month, that my hair was dreadlocked from the sheets and that for the first time since I had Claire I missed two days of work – not from flu or food poisoning but from fucking.

Birthday by Joe Penhall

*You have no concept whatsoever of the pain, of my pain – male
pain – man pain.*

Birthday was first performed at the Royal Court Jerwood Theatre
Downstairs, London, on 22 June 2012. It was directed by Roger Mitchell.

Context

Joe Penhall's tenth play, a black comedy, is all breaking-waters, labour
and hospital beds, but middle-class parenting could not be more unusual,
for it is the man, not the woman, who is giving birth. Penhall presents a
very modern couple who have decided to 'take it in turns' to allow Lisa
to focus on her career, and so it is up to her husband Ed to deliver the
goods this time. Penhall has previously written about parenthood, notably
with *Haunted Child*, which explores the utter devastation of parental
abandonment. There is nothing immaculate about Ed's final trimester;
'How could you forget my f***ing raspberry leaf tea?' he screams.
Penhall presents a delightfully Kafkaesque vision, not only of male
conception, but also the NHS systems that will support and ultimately (in
this case), host the delivery without an anaesthetist! Lisa, his wife, is not
much support either, and why should she be, she bore their first child. It's
payback time. Women don't seem to care much at all really, be it Lisa or
the wonderfully bored registrar, Natasha.

Acting notes

This short comic speech is all about birth and babies, and the utter
loathing of children. Natasha is scared of responsibility and lacks the
maternal instinct that her boyfriend clearly has. Although written in a
familiar, chatty style, the comic thought must be simply constructed and
certainly not played for laughs, which would be indulgent. The speech
will require the sort of preparation a musician might bring to a musical
score. It will need to be marked-up and mapped-out. Comic timing is
not god-given, but the result of rigorous preparation. Natasha doesn't
want children – that much is clear – but the reasons she gives are extraordinary for someone in the medical profession. Her description of how
repulsed she is by the vision of nervous and expectant parents arriving at

the maternity ward is delightfully cynical but so closely observed that it suggests she has thought about what it would be like if it was her and her boyfriend. Is it the pain of birth or the long-term commitment to parenting that so scares her?

Registrar, late twenties

Natasha   I wouldn't have a natural birth if you put a gun to my head. Fuck that for a bunch of bananas. One of the most dangerous, chaotic, stressful things a woman can do. I wouldn't subject my worst enemy to it let alone somebody I loved because, basically, you're playing *Russian roulette*. (*Pause.*) Obstetrics is the most stressful job you can do. I wanted to be a gynaecologist but I couldn't bear the politics – it's a man's world, gynaecology.

Pause as she writes.

Lisa   (Do you have kids?)

Natasha   No, not for me. My boyfriend wants one but after everything I've seen ... no chance, I'm not risking it. He can have it himself. I'll hold his hand.

Lisa   (Don't you want kids?)

Natasha   I don't have any maternal instinct. I don't have a maternal bone in my body. Children annoy me a bit to be honest ... they're so selfish and distracting ... how can you concentrate? (*Pause, writing.*) I feel a bit sorry for people with children ... I can't relate to them ... I see them come in here with their bags packed, all worried and excited, as if they're setting off on some incredible voyage ... to a strange new world ... but they're never coming home.

Black Jesus by Anders Lustgarten

And do you know why I was called by that name? Because I decided who would be saved and who would be condemned. I took that responsibility for others and now I take it for myself. I am Black Jesus. I do not crawl.

Black Jesus received its world premiere at the Finborough Theatre, London, on 1 October 2013. It was directed by David Mercatali.

Context

Zimbabwe in the very near future. Black Jesus, a militia leader called Gabriel Chibamu, is being interviewed by the Truth and Justice Commission about the atrocities of the Mugabe regime. Eunice (from the Commission) asks difficult questions in the knowledge that Chibamu will face trial and must answer to the past. Lustgarten states that his 'intent was to use the play ... to bring up a lot of heavy horrible things that happened in Zimbabwe, things that Zimbabweans themselves lacked the opportunity to talk about'.

Acting notes

Gabriel Chibamu, one the most infamous perpetrators of the horrors of the Mugabe regime, accuses Eunice of raking over his ashes to find things to burn him with, and so ignores her questions. With his justification for his association with the Green Bombers and tales of horrific attacks, Eunice finds that right and wrong, guilt and innocence, are far less clear than she first thought. There is something plausible, almost inevitable, about Gabriel's reasoning, and the story certainly contextualizes his determination and absolute need of 'no going back'. Lustgarten skilfully presents us with the beating heart of a monster and, while not condoning his undoubted bloody past, gives us the space to reflect upon its causes. There is nothing simple; Gabriel's reasoning is as complex as his actions are disturbing. At this point in the play Eunice decides to tell Gabriel about her beloved father, an intellectual and, surprisingly, a supporter of the revolution, who mobilized unemployed youth into the terrifying faction called Green Bombers. Her crucial revelation is twofold: that its original formation had never been designed for violence, but for vocational training, and secondly, that the Truth and Justice Commission had been prevailed upon to alter its recommendations for the treatment of war perpetrators. If Gabriel meets with his victims, his punishment may not be so severe.

Zimbabwean, mid-twenties

Eunice   My father was a thinker.

Gabriel   It is always the intellectuals! Find a shit in the street and I guarantee an intellectual left it behind!

Eunice   He was a quiet, gentle man. Stiff in company, like new shoes. Warm and soft like old slippers with his children. I loved him very much.

He was a supporter of the revolution in the way he knew how. He could not live among the rats and steel bars of the imprisoned, nor the goats and wood smoke of the foot soldiers, but what he could do was think. He designed many of Zanu's best social policies. The Old Man took a shine to him.

As a child, the big men I saw on the television would come to my house and have tea. I thought this was normal, that every child shared a biscuit with Robert Mugabe, that it was something he did when he got bored of his office. He would ask me to fetch him the sugar, and he would let me take a cube from the bowl as a treat, and I felt special, not because I knew who he was but because an adult was paying me attention. My father watched me like a hawk every step of the way, and I will never forget the expression on his face – pride and happiness, but with a bilious green slick of fear over it. I always thought it was my fault, that I was doing something wrong that spoiled his pleasure. But I could never find out what it was.

Those were the good days of Zimbabwe, our days in the sun. Later on, the atmosphere changed and the house grew colder. No more lines of black government cars in the street, their chauffeurs squatting in the drive to throw dice or dominos. No more shared biscuits with the Old Man. I went away to university, but whenever I returned it was to the sound of shouting matches, my mother's voice raised in anger and my father's in defence.

Brief Encounter by Noël Coward, adapted for the stage by Emma Rice

I'm a happily married woman. Or rather I was until a few weeks ago. This is my whole world and it's enough, or rather it was until a few weeks ago.

Emma Rice adapted and directed *Brief Encounter* from an original 1945 screenplay by Noël Coward. His short play, *Still Life*, first produced in 1936, was the inspiration for the film. Kneehigh's production received its world premiere at the Cinema Haymarket, London, on 2 February 2008.

Context

Brief Encounter was originally a one-act play called *Still Life*, written by Noël Coward in the 1930s, and is perhaps far better known as the 1945 iconic black-and-white movie, directed by David Lean, starring Celia Johnson and Trevor Howard, with Rachmaninov's mesmerizing second piano concerto for the sound track. In the film, gorgeous images of trains and sandwich-filled station buffets were saturated with the well-modulated vowel sounds of an adulterously inclined, but trapped, middle class. Both the original play and subsequent film celebrate the impossibility of love that is already taken by another. In both play and movie, the never-to-be couple, Laura and Alec (an ordinary housewife and an ordinary doctor), struggle with the realization that their separately married lives are in some way predetermined and fixed by the social and cultural expectations of polite society. The crippling inaction of their unspoken love at the Milford railway station has lodged (like the famous grit in Laura's eye) into cinema history. Alec will take his family to a new job in South Africa, order will be restored, and never-expressed love will gradually fade. Emma Rice's atmospheric multimedia show was staged in a West End cinema and, whilst the original story remained, Rice added nine Coward songs, nostalgic film sequences and vivid moments of emotional clarity that were absent in the one-act original.

Acting notes

The challenge for the actor is to hold in emotion rather than to display it. The character, Laura, doesn't have the emotional free-spirited repertoire of a liberated woman. She has had to live her emotional life in the abstract and shadowy world of her subconscious – in denial and most certainly in check. She has spent her life pretending to be content and is now experiencing the utterly sterile reality of this fiction. A strange world of emotional surfaces presents itself and she has neither the emotional nor spoken language with which to deal with it. Everything looks and feels different and this makes her feel like a stranger in her own home. Laura is in many ways a two-dimensional figure with a three-dimensional pain. Every thought of hers lacks experience and hope. And so we have a tragic construct whereby the character realizes something utterly pitiful through suffering and inexorable loneliness. But unlike classical tragedy, this poor woman does not die, only her heart does. For those performers who have seen the movie it would be all too easy to put on the posh 1930s voice and play cheap pastiche, but flatness of vowel is about social background, class, experience and choice, not about cliché. It is Laura's inability to communicate her truth and passion that must be communicated in performance.

Laura   Yes it has. I don't want to pretend anything either to you or to anyone else … but from now on I shall have to. That's what's wrong – don't you see? That's what spoils everything. That's why we must stop here and now talking like this. We are neither of us free to love each other, there is too much in the way. There's still time, if we control ourselves and behave like sensible human beings, there's still time to – to …

Alec   There's no time at all.

A **Waiter** *enters with a bottle and two glasses. He pops the cork and pours.*

Laura   Loving you is hard for me – it makes me a stranger in my own house. Familiar things, ordinary things that I've known for years, like the dining room curtains and the wooden tub with the silver top that holds biscuits and the water colour of San Remo that my mother painted, look odd to me, as though they belonged to someone else – when I've just left you, when I go home, I'm more lonely than I've ever been before. I passed the house the other day without noticing and had to turn back, and when I went in it seemed to draw away from me – my whole life seems to be drawing away from me, and – and I don't know what to do. I love them just the same, Fred I mean and the children, but it's as though it wasn't me at all – as though I were looking on at someone else. Do you know what I mean? Is it the same with you? Or is it easier for men –

Can't Forget About You by David Ireland

I mean I know I have only just met but you seem so normal – and
you and your family, and all the other people I meet here, I think
how did any of you manage to grow up normal?

Can't Forget About You received its world premiere at the Lyric Theatre, Belfast, on 19 May 2013. It was directed by Conleth Hill.

Context

Though labelled a 'romantic comedy', *Can't Forget About You* doesn't ever retreat from more urgent themes which include sectarianism, the future of Northern Ireland and cultural identity. We encounter Belfast-born Stevie, a twenty-five-year-old politics graduate, and an older Glaswegian widow, Martha, who rather extraordinarily invites herself into his life and then into his bed ('Would you like to have sex with me?'). This seems to be the perfect solution for it does without the complexities of a long courtship. Martha is not looking for anything long-lasting and neither is Stevie. Or so it seems. But love, not lust, flourishes in the wake of their sexually convenient relationship. The play's knowing humour is both touching and edgy in equal measure – notably the awkward generational exchanges between the much older Martha, younger Stevie and his family. This is difficult territory in that it inhabits the toe-curling truths of an inevitable and exasperated type of cynicism residing within a dysfunctional, difficult relationship where awkward sex not only provokes a set of domestic questions ('And fuck the age difference'), but also agitates by so doing, painful stories from Ireland's past and present.

Acting notes

For someone sleeping with a man many years her junior, Martha appears to be surprisingly naïve. She struggles with her past, her own morality ('all that you should do this, you shouldn't do that'), and the past histories of family and nation. In therapy, older and feeling 'like some haggard old witch', she also struggles to live in the present, being accused by Stevie of constantly talking about her dead husband when she has sex. What is Martha searching for? Why is she unable to identify herself in the present? Is her naïvety genuine or is it some sort of counselled coping strategy? The choices made with such a role are driven by very simple questions. The task would be to identify a simple route through Martha's psychological messy design and measure this alongside her apparent disregard for, or inability to deal with, the actual moment. Is sex on tap with her youthful colt a displacement activity, putting her life on hold, or is it her part of an essential journey towards renewal and a new spiritual beginning?

Glaswegian, forties

Martha   The Troubles.

How we let that happen. Like why it went on. And why it suddenly stopped. And I look around as a stranger here as a, as a lover of this place and the people are so lovely and so friendly and it's unbelievable to me that before I got here you were all blowing each other up!

And I listen to you and – I mean, I know we've only just met but you seem so *normal* – and you and your family, and all the other people I meet here, I think how did any of you manage to grow up normal? How did you manage to live with all that violence in your city for so long and why do you, why do you all seem so lovely and friendly when you lived through *that*? And how could you have done that to each other when you're all so *nice*?

I don't … I don't get it. I don't understand it.

I don't understand how …

She shakes her head in bewilderment

(From later in the play.)

It's just I never grew up with religion. Both my parents were Communists. I did go to Sunday School one time with a friend and – my father was raging about it but my mother thought I should be allowed to go, to make up my own mind. And I remember they told me in Sunday School that if you weren't a Christian, you would go to Hell. And … I don't know … it just seemed unfair, my mother and father were both atheist, so … it seemed wrong of God to send them to Hell when they were good people.

Candide by Mark Ravenhill, inspired by Voltaire

Some time ago I conducted a certain scientific experiment
With a chambermaid.

Candide received its world premiere at the Swan Theatre, Royal Shakespeare Company, Stratford-upon-Avon on 29 August 2013 and was directed by Lyndsey Turner.

Context

Voltaire wrote the novel *Candide* in 1759 in an effort to 'satirise the views' of the philosopher Leibniz, who had stated that life was organized by a grand designer, and who methodically optioned different worlds before putting the human species in the 'the best of all possible worlds'. This is the story of a young aristocrat and his tutor journeying across the world hoping to prove that, in spite of human cruelty and natural disaster, 'everything is for the best'. Ravenhill uses a dramatic structure which shifts between the eighteenth and twenty-first centuries with scenes set in the past, present and near-future.

Acting notes

The first of two the speeches selected from this play is a disturbing vision of the future that looks to a time when fresh water is so scarce that it has become the centre-piece to war. As ever with Ravenhill's work, the character Sophie seems deceptively straightforward, almost easy on the page, but the challenge here is to actually reveal the post-apocalyptic tone of Sophie's prophesy, as well as, crucially, authenticate or humanize her terrifying perspective, for it is spoken by a young girl to her mother. Is the daughter trying to shock her mother for some reason? Who has she learnt this information from? Children generally understand how their parents consider the world; has the mother heard all this before and neglected to respond, or is this a one-off vision that the daughter feels compelled to share? For this speech not assume the chaotic unreality of the nightmare spectrum, where facts and logic have no place or currency, the performer will have to plot through the girl's need to state that she will walk into any room with a gun and shoot.

The second speech is that of Cunegonde, who actually speaks a sort of politically-charged but very personal rhetoric, fused with quite extraordinary visual and sensual language ('I kept both sides warm between my legs'). She waits for Candide and her waiting takes a lifetime. The challenge is, as with the other extraordinary speech from this play, how to humanize her experience, while fully realizing the incredible impact of Ravenhill's potent language. How can the performer enable this encounter with Cunegonde go beyond being merely a wordy historical reverie?

Sophie   Oh Mummy! Sorting through your rubbish?
Separating green and brown glass?
Wind turbines?
There was a tipping point: it's tipped.
Ozone's blasted through
Sun is pouring in
Ice melting
Water's rising
And you're pissing in the wind.
Have you actually read the science?
Nature is fighting, clear us away.
Once we're gone
The planet's going to be just fine.
But the people –
Here's the problem:
Our race keeps on getting bigger
Seven billion now
How long before we're ten, fifteen, twenty billion?
But the portion of the earth
That will be inhabitable
As it all heats up
Much smaller
Maybe enough for a three, four billion.
In my lifetime
There's going to be millions upon millions moving up the hemisphere –
From southern Spain at first, then whole continents
All demanding to live here,
A cooler climate.
What we going to do?
Gun towers on every beach?
Reservoirs will be guarded by armies.
You've seen wars for oil, right?
Wait 'til the water wars begin.
So it's kinder, better, saner, to start the culling of the human race today
That's why I say to everyone
Do the same as me:
Get a gun, walk into a room – any room –
And shoot.

Cunegonde   Listen:
I cried for bread and liberty
The King fled
We stormed the Bastille
Dance for the Republic
Liberté! Egalité! Fraternité!
Kiss me.
I called for my brother's execution
I dropped the guillotine
Felt the blood on my lip
Tasted good
Ever optimistic
One day Candide will kiss me.
Kiss me.
Turned on every comrade I ever had
Order must be restored
(For Candide's kiss)
I kept both sides warm between my legs
Gave birth a hundred and forty-three times
Miscarried many more
(Look what it's done to my body)
Kiss me
Fed half my boys to the war machine
Most of the girls – a life of quiet servitude
One day Candide will kiss me
Kiss me
Put up barricades
Seige
Optimism comrades
Woman put down your broom! Listen:
Optimism
(I'm waiting for Candide's kiss)
Kiss me
I worked without light
Factory
Mine
Rowing the ship of my own slavery
We sang songs
Optimism
Optimism
Optimism
Kiss me

I set out around the globe
Classify every plant, species, being
A great catalogue
Killed much of what I found
And still the catalogue awaits completion.
My lover was a dictator
Genocide designer
I stood beside him
(One day Candide will kiss me)
Kiss me

Cannibals by Rory Mullarkey

The world's not overflowing you know. There isn't enough, woman.
It's dog eat dog, and living means taking from others. You'd take
from them and then just let it go to waste? Eat up.

Cannibals received its world premiere at the Royal Exchange Theatre,
Manchester, on 3 April 2013 and was directed by Michael Longhurst.

Context

Rory Mullarkey's first full-length play is set in a war-destroyed, desolate
post-Soviet region where eating is living. Eating anything. The play has
a sort of *King Lear* timelessness to it – it could be set in ancient times or
some terrible time in our future. A place of ghosts, madmen, soldiers and
the hungry. The central character, Lizaveta, barely exists in this war-torn
landscape by farming potatoes and enduring many hardships by talking
to a mad icon painter. This is a harsh place with the need for harsh acts of
survival. Lizaveta describes her life in mostly broken shards of language,
which strangely collapse not into silence but into extended folkloric
tales of the past and her hopes for the future. All is dramaturgically set,
it seems, for something resembling the nightmare vision of playwright
Howard Barker or Edward Bond. But then, without warning, something
quite extraordinary occurs. Lizaveta is kidnapped, taken away from this
post-apocalyptic world and driven in the boot of a car to Manchester.
Waking up in a hotel room she meets a man she has never met before –
her new husband.

Acting notes

This speech occurs a little before Lizaveta is taken to Manchester. It is
almost hallucinatory in that, whilst it lists things that she can remember,
it is its near poetic rhythm, its use of the repetition, 'I remember', and its
utter strangeness that give a sort of fairy-tale wash to the narrative. Her
memory is sensual and located within vivid moments of nature – the trees
and sky are a constant but changing, background to her ever-developing,
but sparse, life. Sensuality becomes sordid sexuality, her abused life now
the convenience of a nameless man who touches her when he is ready
to touch her. This is a truly difficult play. Its themes are disturbing and

their articulation dependent on an unsentimental and non-demonstrative playing style. What should shock is not the extraordinariness of the actor in the moment of performance, but the everydayness of the character's awful plight. The actor must not indulge in every grisly aspect – the character's bit-by-bit, horrible life laid bare – but must explore such degradation as a living norm. It is only us, the audience, who will sense the atrocity. For Lizaveta, the extreme experiences of her life are driven by the near-animal instincts of a trapped creature sensing death. How does the actor humanize and own the big themes within a little beating heart? This is the challenge.

Lizaveta   Okay. (*The speech has a pace of its own, and she starts slowly.*) I was born on a farmstead about four days' walk from here. I don't know how long ago. For some reason, no one told me it was important to keep count. I don't remember too much about my parents, except that my mother was tall and my father was short. From my childhood I remember lying outside in the shade in the forest, looking up at some branches above my head. I remember throwing a ball. I remember running down a track. I remember falling, cutting my leg and the palms of my hands, crying. I remember nights when I was scared of the dark and I couldn't sleep. I remember thinking it was darker in the room than when I closed my eyes. I remember a bull, a big one, snorting at me as I passed its field on the way to the well. I remember my baby brother dying and helping my father to dig a hole at the far end of our field. I remember my mother crying in the night. I remember thinking it might be selfish of me to be reassured by her crying but it stopped me being scared of the dark. I remember a man coming to the house and talking to my parents. I remember he smelled of potatoes and that he left. I remember he came back again and took me with him to a farm on the other side of the valley. I remember the farm on the other side of the valley was exactly the same as mine except smaller and on the other side of the valley. I remember he picked me up in his arms threw me up up up and down onto the bed. I remember he promised not to touch me until I was older. I remember he kept his promise, and I was glad. I remember he showed me how to chop vegetables and to feed the chickens. I remember he watched me milking the cows. I remember he told me my parents were dead now and I only had him, but that felt okay. I remember eventually he did touch me in the night and it hurt at first and then it didn't and then it did again. I didn't bleed and then I did and then I didn't.

Casualties by Ross Ericson

*So what? So what if he was a dog? It could have been any of us. I
was on the other side of that wall when that thing went up. I stood
there and watched as lumps of burnt flesh landed all around me.*

Casualties received its world premiere at the Park Theatre, London, on 18
June 2013 and was directed by Harry Burton.

Context

Afghanistan. A counter IED team deal with keeping the peace and holding
their nerve. In the introduction to the play, playwright Ross Ericson (who
briefly served in the military) states that when he 'saw these brave young
lads on the news, telling us that they were 'just doing their job', and that
they were just going to 'crack on', I am sorry to say I did not believe them.
They were saying what was expected of them, what had been drilled
into them, and I was sure they, and their stoically supportive families,
did not fully understand what was really ahead.' In a significant moment
at the start of *Casualties*, we encounter soldiers Gary and Mike on the
night before their return to service in Afghanistan and the bomb disposal
team. They strangely observe that Helmand province might actually be
a more attractive proposition than their war-affected broken home life.
We then cut to a riveting extended sequence of short intercut scenes
where the parallel lives of Gary and Mike, and their utterly bleak military
existence, is graphically and tragically exposed. For those women at
home, connected with the IED team, a different battle is very apparent.
Their fragile lives are in a constant state of anxiety and waiting. It is as if
Ross Ericson makes no distinction between their bravery and that of the
men at war.

Acting notes

The speech exists in the closed down emotional landscape of shock and
mourning. Emma's thoughts are very slow and difficult in formation; her
ideas are narrow in focus. The wideness of her world is all but gone. She
describes an administrative error that had such devastating consequences
for a widowed friend of hers. The friend accidentally found out about
her husband's death when she opened an unclaimed army services wages

letter sent to her by mistake. The letter stated that her husband hadn't completed a full month's service at the time of his death and therefore his wages would be reduced. It is the telling of this very unfortunate story that triggers Emma's own memories of recent loss. In the speech there is no screaming or wailing, just an extraordinarily matter-of-fact acceptance of what has happened to both her and her friend. In any audition, it would be tempting to seize this type of speech as the perfect opportunity to demonstrate lots of emotional range, but Emma's grief has no range. All is reduced and broken. The quiet tragedy of this monologue is its ordinariness. The memory of Emma's husband weighs heavy, and she is barely able to reveal anything about herself because all emotion has necessarily been locked away. This is not a play about heroes, but a story about those who are left. Emma's emptiness and absence of thought determines the thinking tempo. At this point, all is about the moment-by-moment need to continue, however difficult that might be. She is not at a point where she can actually piece together her own personal tragedy and so attempts to process what has happened by reflecting on someone else's story. The significant challenge in this speech is that the flatness of her psychological moment must be realized in a theatrically relevant and truthful way.

Gary's wife, in her mid-thirties, works for a bank

Emma   About a month after Crabby's funeral she appeared on my doorstep in floods of tears. Why she came to me I'll never know, we were never exactly close. Anyway, it turned out that that morning she got a letter from the army. She showed it to me. It was all very matter-of-fact, saying that there was some wages owed due to unclaimed leave and that this would be paid into her account within the next seven days. Nothing to cry about really, but then they added underneath that three hundred and forty nine pounds and fifty eight pence would be deducted because Crabby had not completed a full month service since his last pay date. Three hundred and forty nine pounds and fifty eight pence deducted because he had inconveniently died before the end of the month. I suppose when they told her they were indebted to Crabby for his sacrifice she didn't realise that there would be deductions. Three hundred and forty nine pounds and fifty eight pence, his life wasn't even worth that to them.

Pause.

Peter   How is Staff ...

Pause.

Funny, there's still a moment in the morning, a few seconds when I first wake up, that I actually forget what's happened. I roll over in bed and when I find he's not there I just think, it's alright, he's away, he'll be home soon. But then I see the padre and Major Thorn on the doorstep, with their serious uniforms and their serious faces, and I remember. It's like a great black sickness that rises up from my guts and wraps itself around me, and I see him lying on that bed all ... all torn up with tubes sticking out of him and ... Sorry. You said something about having some questions?

City Love by Simon Vinnicombe

I feel like asking him to stay. To never leave this room. But I know that son he will leave and ...

City Love received its world premiere at the CLF Art Café, Bussey Building, Peckham Rye on 10 September 2013 and was directed by Sarah Bedi.

Context

Simon Vinnicombe's two-hander is remarkable in that it is an old-fashioned, boy-meets-girl romance but with very contemporary issues. Vinnicombe's characters play out storybook moments more typically seen via Hollywood's vision of London in love – the breathless first encounter that leads us through anticipation, passion and joy to the inevitable everyday problems that can all too easily fracture and destroy a relationship. The play presents a sequence of sometimes heart-wrenching extended monologues.

Acting notes

The acting challenge in both speeches from this play is quite clear. Such storytelling certainly requires a performance style that doesn't inadvertently collapse into the easy cliché of *Four Weddings and a Funeral* textbook 'rom-com' method – all sighs and sad looks. Lovers and loving are often played as simple truths. The trap for any actor is not to accidentally play character with a single focus or straight-lined inner life, one that is just in or out of love. How will the dishes get washed or the bills get paid? How will the inner joys of partnership be met alongside the nagging doubts of union? Presenting young love as dramatic subject matter is potentially quite dull to watch, for it is actually a quite ordinary (and lovely) experience. Finding the tension between inner doubts, fears and confusions, alongside the blind overwhelming experience of loving and being loved is the challenge. The staging of the original production was very simple with the actors perched on separate boxes, only to meet in the middle when in love and to separate when out of it. This simplicity should give a clear sense of performance style but it does not give immediate solutions to dangers of acting someone 'in lerv'. A strong dynamic inner world of questions and doubts will need to be constructed.

Contemporary London, mid-twenties

Lucy   I'm in trouble now you see?

I'm better on my own.

That's what works for me. I'm not unhappy. I'm happy. Really.

§

So I go a little bit giddy these days at the thought of him. Hearing him. Seeing him. It's a sugar rush. First burst of spring, when you uncoil yourself from the utter misery of January and February and the sun bursts through. City parks filled with optimistic lunch-eaters. Drinks outside bars on streets. Walking on the canal to work even though it takes half an hour longer. And with hummingbirds in your belly and this odd sense of warmth that lifts your whole body.

He wears this jacket. All the time. With a wool lining. It cups his jaw, brushes his smile. His legs are so long. His walk.

The weight of his chest when he moves into me.

There's something in his eyes. He looks like he'll look after me. And I know that's not very New Age. I know I'm letting Germain down but I want to be looked after. And I want someone to look after too. What's wrong with that?

And what's wrong with wanting him to ring?

Every second of every day.

What's wrong with that?

I stayed at his for the first time. We just talked. There was never any sense of …

Talking all through the night.

He had put toothpaste on a new toothbrush for me when I went into the bathroom.

I think I'm supposed to feel owned or belittled or. But it just makes me melt.

Contemporary London, mid-twenties

Lucy   I don't want to ring him. I don't want to speak to him.

But I think about it every minute of every day. I think about him.

Frightened of what comes next.

She stares down at her phone. She gazes at it as though it were almost an instrument of torture.

I believe in preparation. It's what I do very well at work.

So I will just write things to say on the phone. In case I get a bit stuck or the conversation doesn't flow or my mouth dries and I feel like an eight-year-old kiss-chaser who doesn't know how to talk to a boy.

She starts to write things down on a pad.

(*Writes.*) 'What you been up to this week?'

'Have you been talking to any strange women in bus stops lately' … That's even less funny written down.

'I thought I'd ring.'

Oh dear lord!

No.

She starts typing on her phone.

I decided … that I couldn't get enough words in a text … and more than one text always seems a little bit … needy.

She smiles. Pleased with that. Continues to type.

Get nervous on the phone and never say anything I want to.

An email can be drafted and still come out this bad!

I had a lovely time the other night … I'm sorry I've taken two days to respond. My friends had a big talk to me about the number of days I should wait to respond … There was no consensus … other than ringing you the next morning would make me a bunny boiler with no life. I don't understand any of this by the way!

You should know that I wanted to ring you the minute you walked away from the bus stop.

My friends will kill me for telling you that.

So … In short … I'd like to go out with you sometime. Very much.

Clean by Sabrina Mahfouz

*I got mugged when I was fourteen – for a Nokia you could just
about play Sanke on and a Karen Millen bag with a dress in it for
my mum's birthday*

Clean received its world premiere at the Traverse Theatre, Edinburgh, on
14 August 2013 and was part of the Traverse's Breakfast Plays season at
the Edinburgh Festival. It was directed by Orla O'Loughhlin.

Context

Sabrina Mahfouz is a British Egyptian poet and playwright who describes
her theatre as mainly coming from poetry that she has 'written first'. *Clean*
starts with a scene-setting audio narration, where a woman called Sabrina
states that she 'met a man who wrote the stories for some very well-
known computer games, and asks, "how come all the female characters
were so rubbish in these games?"' She then describes how she set about
writing a tale of three females 'who could easily be the basis of crime-
based computer games'. Zainab, Chloe and Katya step forward; their
club-land lives sprawl across a huge gangster-filled canvass of private
jets, warehouse meetings and terrifying ex-Soviet states 'far from home'.
'I had 48 hours to write Clean,' says Mahfouz. 'It was performed at such
a fast pace that when we went to New York as part of Brits on Broadway,
I think a lot of people found it difficult to understand.' Zainab, Chloe and
Katya – London's best 'clean' criminals and perpetrators of 'victimless'
crime – are forced together as an unlikely trio – will they win the game?

Acting notes

The setting, like much of Mahfouz's work is theatrically sparse, with
no set and only basic props required. This allows for an immediate,
very physical performance style, the performer necessarily creating the
worlds and people described. The main task for the performer is clear
– the many shards of thought have to cohere within an internal logic,
however seemingly abstract or extreme. Zainab is like an avatar, whose
comic-book life takes us to places and contexts more usually flicked-to-
life on a GameBoy or computer terminals. In this speech Zainab takes
us to a 'mostly white' restaurant, where she waits in the VIP section on

the second floor. Her description is vivid and tense. This is a place of pleasure but not a place to ever relax in. The restaurant owner has put her 'in a good place', spaced so that she 'can like, check out the faces'. Zainab, forever monitoring, forever checking and making sure. What is she scared of?

Zainab   The restaurant is like, mostly white. There are some neon bits of brightly coloured wall, no windows so you dunno if it's night or day. But it's mostly night.

The people who are dining here are mostly right and they all seem to be of a strangely similar height. The club that I been doing business in for a year or so now, the club that I love, the club where I near enough live, is just there, through the restaurant back door.

This place is one of them ones that has never had to throw out a punter for fighting before and the lobby's lighting fixture cost much more than some people in some countries sell their sisters for, serious. The man who opens the door is mostly someone who worked for the royal family once before. I'm sitting on the VIP second floor as I know one of the owners, who mostly owns football teams that never score – but he wanted a place to entertain and so he did what most people with too much money do and opened a restaurant stroke club which is mostly white for people who are mostly right and all seem to be of a, like, strangely similar height.

Right now, my business date is late. The owner's put me in a good place though, spaced so I can like, check out the faces on display. I'm mainly checking these two clean-crime ladies, that's my category as well, clean crime – meaning no death no blood no mess kinda ting but still illegal as sin.

Anyways, I see these two, Chloe and Katya, but they ain't seen me. Which is how it should be, cos I ain't one of them ones who wants to be seen. Not like that Chloe, gleaming all over with diamonds and shit like someone's gonna find that discreet. She treats people like they ain't worth her words – I mean, I never met her, but I heard. And I can see the way her back so straight in her chair, is like she trying so hard to get her nose higher in the air. Yeh, she ain't subtle boy. But I hear she's good at what she does so I ain't fussing, just, I'd never be trusting someone who wore their work round their neck, ya get me?

The Curious Incident of the Dog in the Night Time by Mark Haddon, adapted for the stage by Simon Stephens

I wanted to come and tell you that I didn't kill Wellington. And also I want to find out who killed him.

The Curious Incident of the Dog in the Night Time was originally produced at the Cottesloe at the National Theatre, on 24 July 2012. It was directed by Marianne Elliott.

Context

Christopher is trying to find out who killed next-door's dog with a garden fork. He is trying to find out because he is the prime suspect. His father isn't keen on any investigation and his mother left him years ago, so doesn't seem to care. Christopher presses ahead but the problem is that he has never been further than the end of his street. His investigations take him on a frightening journey that finds answers to questions that he had never even thought of. This is not simply a story of a boy with Asperger's syndrome, but a sometimes bleak, sometimes heart-warming, meditation on the nature of family, truth and friendship. Stephens structures the dramatic narrative with almost magic-realist beauty; scenes dissolve, characters transform and become others, and the reality of love and living is constantly questioned. The prodigy uncovers almost unbearable answers to equations that don't appear in his maths book.

Acting notes

Christopher's mother tries to explain why she has been absent in his life and seeks forgiveness. She suggests that if things had been different, and if he had been different, she might have been a better mother. This is a tough revelation, one that would be extremely difficult for any parent. The problem is that however well-meaning her words are, she still doesn't appreciate or understand that her son will not be able to fully respond to this openness because of his condition. Her seemingly heartfelt words are all but wasted. Why, knowing this to be the case, does Judy continue to speak the way that she does? In another section of the play, we hear a letter she writes, explaining similar feelings. The performer must not construct the easy binary that she is either a 'good' or 'bad' mother. Her description of the terrible episode in Bentalls store, one that has clearly haunted her, reveals mixed but ultimately shameful memories of her early attempts at parenting. It seems that she ran away from her responsibility to her child, but cannot escape the torment of such an action. The performer has a terrific opportunity in this speech to create the vivid images of the Bentalls shopping trip, with all its awkward stares and blushed apologies, but the real test would be to try to wire her psychological reasoning as a mother. What is her need? Why does she explain, in such detail, an event that Christopher probably can't remember? Was the trip the emotional trigger for her departure or was it actually that her relationship with his father was broken before that point? The speech could easily be a heart-rending cry for help but equally it could also be seen as a crassly inappropriate action by an adult to a vulnerable child.

Judy   Dear Christopher. I said that I wanted to explain to you why I went away when I had the time to do it properly. Now I have lots of time. So I'm sitting on the sofa here with this letter and the radio on and I'm going to try and explain.

I was not a very good mother Christopher. Maybe if things had been different, maybe if you'd been different, I might have been better at it. But that's just the way things turned out.

I'm not like your father. Your father is a much more patient person. He just gets on with things and if things upset him he doesn't let it show.

But that's not the way I am and there's nothing I can do to change it.

Do you remember once when we were shopping in town together? And we went into Bentalls and it was really crowded and we had to get a Christmas present for Grandma? And you were frightened because of all the people in the shop. It was the middle of Christmas shopping when everyone was in town. And I was talking to Mr Land who works on the kitchen floor and went to school with me. And you crouched down on the floor and put your hands over your ears and you were in the way of everyone so I got cross because I don't like shopping at Christmas either, and I told you to behave and I tried to pick you up and move you. But you shouted and you knocked those mixers off the shelf and there was a big crash. And everyone turned round to see what was going on and Mr Land was really nice about it but there were boxes and bits of string and bits of broken bowl on the floor and everyone was staring and I saw that you had wet yourself and I was so cross and I wanted to take you out of the shop but you wouldn't let me touch you and you just lay on the floor and screamed and banged your hands and feet on the floor and the manager came and asked me what the problem was and I was at the end of my tether and I had to pay for two broken mixers and we just had to wait until you stopped screaming. And then I had to walk you all the way home, which took hours because I knew you wouldn't go on the bus again.

Dark Vanilla Jungle by Philip Ridley

I was stung by a wasp once – Shall I tell you about this? Well, it's something you don't know. And I have to start somewhere.

Dark Vanilla Jungle received its world premiere at Pleasance Courtyard, Edinburgh, on Wednesday 31 July 2013. It was directed by David Mercatali.

Context

In this one-woman play, the increasingly distracted Andrea, 15, bursts into a relentless confession. She has never been told that she is beautiful. The insignificant teenage ramblings slowly give way to something much more vivid, real and horrific. Her pitiful life is described through a sequence of apparently random moments, innocent at first, with Cheryl Wignall, who 'had more gums than teeth', wasps and music festivals, and a delightfully un-heroic list of other normal people such as her mum. But then she meets a man from the local McDonald's. This is not a comic turn, but a dark painful one infused with utter misery and loss – an urban nightmare. Back at McDonald's, Andrea and a girl called Emma are convinced by older men to go clubbing, the two innocent girls, now being tragically drawn into a most disturbing regime. Andrea's former life, of simple random encounters collapses, as she becomes a fully 'groomed' girl made for the pleasure of men.

Acting notes

The speech contains some achingly lyrical moments – 'I've pulled the green curtains all round the cubicle. If I half close my eyes I could be in a field of long grass.' The performer will have to work hard not for her words to be engulfed by the overarching sense of the play and its miserable tone and manner. The performer must be alert to the fact that Andrea is not as aware of her desperate plight. The emotional impact of her suffering is therefore dependent on localizing her young thought and experience to a simple state of not knowing or understanding. Thoughts and memories must therefore be very diligently explored and plotted, for if the speech is just played for effect it will appear indulgent and emotionally dull. To judge or feel sorry for her life would be to reduce the living experience of it.

Andrea   Hospitals sound wonderful, don't you think. All the hushed voices and electric beeps. There's something soothing about it all. If only I'd known sooner, I'd've come more often. They've been very kind to me. I've had three cups of tea.

One while I was waiting in A&E with Mrs Vye and two while I've been in here. It's a side ward or something. There's five cubicles but all the others are empty. They've taken Mrs Vye to have a scan. They said I could go with her if I wanted but I said I'd rather not. That's when I got my third cup of tea. A male nurse brought it. He was balding and had bright red cheeks. I could see him looking at my breasts. I think he's very lonely. He probably lives by himself. A mummy's boy and mummy died recently. I've pulled the green curtains all round the cubicle. If I half close my eyes I could be in a field of long grass – Oh! Someone's being put in the next bed. I'm being nudged through the curtain. I move my seat to give them more room. I can hear the nurse who wants to suck my nipples. And there's the doctor who told me Mrs Vye's had a massive stroke and I should expect the worst. He's called Doctor Zinta. He has a lovely accent. I bet his home's full of books and statues of elephants – Who's that talking now? It's a new voice. A woman. She talking about … her son! He's the one who's ill. He's … he's got … what's that? Speak up, woman. An infection! I get nudged again. How much space do people want? This was a relaxing field of grass before they turned up. The nurse and doctor call the woman Renee. They talk like old friends. The son's obviously a regular here …

Dirty Great Love Story by Richard Marsh and Katie Bonna

For the first time in see
My newly single future
Cheering and leering before me.

Dirty Great Love Story received its world premiere at the Pleasance Theatre, Edinburgh, in August 2012. It was directed by Pia Furtado.

Context

Dirty Great Love Story started life in 2010 as a ten-minute light-romantic poem that explored how two people cope with the hopes and disappointments of love. The play presents the same two poetic lovers, Rich and Katie, who although both terribly enthusiastic for love, find themselves single and at the wrong end of twenty. One evening, drunk, decidedly un-poetic and accidentally together, they become a couple. In the morning and days that follow, their relationship is made vulnerable by the very unromantic problems of everyday life, with many bad jokes, spectacular misunderstandings, ridiculous and interfering friends, and general bad relationship management. Sober, the lovers question their night of passion and whether the extraordinary coincidence of their meeting was luck or just very bad timing.

Acting notes

The speech is ostensibly a tough statement about contemporary love, given in candid good humour, by a woman who has yet to find it. But on closer reading, it reveals just how vulnerable and alone she is, with the word 'need' used at least five times, alongside other repetitive phrases of desperation and heartbreak. Is Katie's 'messed up heart' a symptom of something slightly darker and disturbing or is she just unlucky? When Katie kisses a stranger, she wants to 'forget about everything'; why is this? What is she trying to forget? The performer must piece together the many seemingly light references to past encounters, and see that, on this occasion, her feet are in shreds and her rejected flesh is crawling. The speech opens with her very casual 'need to keep laughing', but it would seem that Katie has very little joy in her life, and until she confronts the reasons why she is like this, will not escape the awful cycle of heartbreak and despair.

Somewhere around thirty years old

Katie   Need to keep laughing,
Maybe I'll lean in,
Maybe I'll have this Mr Priest.
Even though his voice is annoying,
Like a seal who went to Eton.
I kiss him and forget everything …
Shit, I thought Rich was over there.
Screw him, Matt's hot and he's here.
Shots mount,
Flesh shouts,
Booze bout,
Lose count,
Lips pounce …
I wake up in the coatroom,
Spooning the space where Matt slept –
Or didn't bother to before he left.
Recover underwear,
Ripped off and flung into dust-coated corners.
Flee into the pre-ignition still of morning.
Need to keep eyes down,
Need to keep walking,
Need to keep rejected flesh from crawling,
Need to stop stomach lining falling
To the platform.
Watching train after train after train depart.
My feet cut to shreds from being dressed up,
Just like my messed-up heart.

A Doll's House by Henrik Ibsen, English language version by Simon Stephens

I think I'm a human being before anything else. I don't care what other people say. I don't care what people write in books. I need to think for myself.

This adaptation of *A Doll's House* received its world premiere at the Young Vic Theatre, London, on 29 June 2012. It was directed by Carrie Cracknell.

Context

Ibsen's timeless exploration of truth, money and spiritual freedom has had many famous revivals and translations, but Stephens presents a new English version which is more like a thriller than a dusty classic. Wife and mother, Nora is dangerously close to madness when she realizes that she must escape her marriage or be forever without hope. The play's forceful exploration of Nora's destruction was hugely controversial when first published in 1879, and seems to have much the same impact today. Nora and Torvald would seem to be happily married but Nora has a secret debt, and their relationship crumbles under the pressure of the interrogation of lies and truths that dance around this fact. Although Torvald forgives her, he is ultimately abandoned by his wife, who realizes that he has used her like a doll. Nora claims to be unfit to be a mother or wife, and Ibsen's final stage direction is that of the door closing behind her. The brilliance of this desolate, fragile moment is that Nora's impossible dilemma – to stay trapped, used and unfulfilled, or to leave her family and find a new relevant life – is humanized and exists beyond gender.

Acting notes

Nora is trapped in a loveless marriage and believes that her life is becoming evermore difficult to live. She fears that unless she does something quite dramatic, there is very little possibility of escape, and in a ponderous, distracted exchange with Kristine, thinks aloud, about her life and what it has come to. Although very early in the play, Nora's decision to leave her husband and family is clearly evidenced in this speech. There is a sense of her plotting and preparing, of working things out; her mind is racing with different thoughts about her future. She also describes how her marriage is tied to a ticking time-bomb, of youthful good looks that will fade, and feminine appeal that will pass. She is under no illusion; it is her 'little performances' and dances that have kept her marriage together. The longer sentences at the start of the speech are very different in structure to those shorter ones at the end. Why is this?

Nora   Is it foolish to save your husband's life?

Kristine, he wasn't allowed to know anything. He wasn't even allowed to know just how ill he really was. The doctors spoke to me, not him. They told me his life was in danger. They told me that the only thing that could save him was a trip away from the darkness and the cold here and down into the South. I had to discover a way of persuading him to leave without him ever knowing how ill he was. I told him how jealous I was of all the other wives who travelled abroad with their husbands. It was his job to look after me. I cried. I begged. He had to indulge me. I suggested he borrow some money. He got so angry. He told me that his only real duty as a husband was not to give in to my little whims and moods. But I needed to save him. I needed to find another way.

Kristine   Did your father never –

Nora   He died before he ever knew.

Kristine   And you've never admitted anything to Torvald?

Nora   How could I? He would be so embarrassed. He would be humiliated.

Kristine *looks at* **Nora**.

Some time.

Kristine   Will you ever tell him, do you think?

Nora   Oh, maybe one day. When I'm old. And tired and haggard. When I'm not quite as beautiful as I am now. I'm being serious. When he's stopped enjoying watching me dance for him. And dressing for him. When he no longer cares about my little performances for him. It would be a good thing to have a little secret up my sleeve.

What am I talking about? That'll never happen.

Dry Ice by Sabrina Mahfouz

The kind of type to make you question how much you really want
to continue this life as he rifles through pinstriped pockets, writes
his number on a dry-cleaning docket and reckons you're friends
now cos when you bent over and he touched your thigh you didn't
tell security to do him in.

Nominated at The Stage Awards for Best Solo, *Dry Ice* received its world premiere at the Underbelly Cowgate, Edinburgh, on 4 August 2011 and was part of the Edinburgh Fringe Festival. It was directed by David Schwimmer.

Context

Sabrina Mahfouz is a British Egyptian poet and playwright who describes her theatre as mainly coming from poetry that she has 'written first'. The dream-like surreal world of Dry Ice, with its magical rapid-fire mix of poetical and political styles is both extraordinarily theatrical – for it requires the solo performer to create many different people and settings, and austere, for it is written to be performed on a bare stage with just a single chair. It follows the character Nina, a stripper, whose complex life we share for a couple of hours: we see her getting ready for a night out; at a dinner-party with P, her half art-dealer, half drug-dealer, boyfriend; and finally, going to work. Nina recounts the complex and often disturbing moments of her life with near-lyrical ease. Mahfouz, who worked as a waitress in strip clubs for several years before writing this play, questions the reality of women's supposed free-choice in relation to the roles they are actually given in society, and the roles that they give themselves.

The bulge in his pocket – wads of fifties or evidence of over-
average virility? Who can say? Except for the girl he choses
for his sit-down. His hour of private whore. Of private dance
and private talk.

Acting notes

Nina's chaotic life is told with the use of just simple theatrical props, a single chair and bare stage. The world that Mahfouz creates is full of extreme characters and situations that, though seemingly theatrical, must not be reduced to dramatic cliché. The many roles that seep in and out of Nina's narration should not appear to be like cheap turns – with voices and movements to match. Her world is colonized by violence, addiction, desperation and little hope. The foul-mouthed men, sleazy locations, danger and loneliness of this woman's life will all require physical embodiment. This is virtuoso stuff, but it should not be seen as such, for the worlds of *Dry Ice* are dimly lit, casual and harrowing.

In the first speech Nina describes in scene one how she had never told her mother that she was going to become a stripper. She describes the type of men who go to strip clubs, 'The Regular Lads', or those with 'mouth open' and 'pleading'. The presence of the men is ever-close, with their interjections voices by the performer, who must simultaneously interact with the men that populate the clubs. Nina doesn't judge, but merely presents their crude, drunken or drug-fuelled behaviour; and in so doing, the performer must realize their inner motives for if not the characters will become cartoonic. The speech is not cabaret, but the presentation of the grotesque extremes of unseen worlds made now visible.

In the second speech, in scene two, Nina describes a dinner-party with her partner P, where 'the table bends in the middle with the weight of the New Wave Heal's plates'. Nina, bored by the company, describes an encounter she once had with a 'wholesome' stripper, her face 'full of flirty smiles'. The story is extraordinary – part magical, the stripper turns-out to be a mermaid, and part ridiculous, Nina is seeing how far the assembled men will believe her tale. The speech is technically challenging, for the description of the mermaid is sensual and clear, but the performer must also signal Nina's growing awareness of ensnaring those listening, bit by bit, with an evermore fabricated account of this 'motherly figure full of tea'. What forms Nina's inner justification? Joy at spinning a good yarn, or the utter loathing of those listening to it?

Nina   I mean, right or wrong, I'd never told my mum that I was going to become a stripper.

I just didn't think it was a career that would hit her as something to tell the neighbours about, no matter how much they loved Nicole from the Pussycat Dolls.

Oh, if I had of told her, then the accusing look on her face would have been a thousand times worse than P's had just been.

Actually, this vision, of my mum's God-fearing, accusing face, was pretty much all I could see when I made it to the club for my first night of 'exotic dancing'.

(Although I learnt early on that dancing is the smallest part of the show and the money's where your fingers go.)

On that first night I was so scared. I had fun though and pretty much met all the types I would meet over the next four years.

Lemme tell ya about them.

So. Number one and most abundant are 'The Regular Lads' Lads', most of whom proudly announce themselves as dads' and have photos of their little, sweet Maisie in their wallets which they flash shamelessly as they take out their Visa Debit to pay for your last naked, wet twenty minutes.

They're there with their friends, they'll claim.

'Our wives know it's the thing to do on a night out – Christ, they got into the trend of pole-dancing classes down the gym so they can't exactly whip our arses for enjoying the expertise of a proper striptease, can they darlin'?'

Course not, no.

'But bloody hell, it is a shame about the price. Any chance of a two for one ahaha.'

Knobs. And worth avoiding at most costs.

Number two type.

The number two type was, due to my judgemental stereotyping mind, the one I was already most familiar with – but of course he really does exist.

Sweat in beads at the back of a fat neck peering jeerily out of a starched white shirt which alerts everyone but the wearer to the jut-out belly like a cut-out copy of a cartoon family guy.

Mouth open with grunts and pleadings for you to '*lean in a bit closer sweet thing, yeh, wag those fun bags right here*' as his tongue licks slippy lips you can avoid his puffed-lid eyes by staring into the inside of his smoky black mouth, like the inside of a burnt-out building that's been flash backed, glowing cinders now fat with hardened ash which the squatter smoking blowbacks scrapes aside.

The kind of type to make you question how much you really want to continue this life as he rifles through pinstriped pockets, writes his number on a dry-cleaning docket and reckons you're friends now cos when you bent over and he touched your thigh you didn't tell security to do him in so now he grins and tells you '*You're a good girl int ya, a naughty good girl*'.

Curls his finger round the score you charge and ignores the fact that you're retching like a car engine at the very sight of him.

Although to be fair, depending how much I've been drinking, I sometimes think 'ah poor thing'.

But that's only til he brings his clientele over, says that you'll bowl them over and probably let them get hand happy if they tip you an extra ten. Ten! Then raises eyebrows at you secretly, like he's just struck you a deal Rodinio or someone would be happy with. Prick.

The third type: The In-Betweeners.

The squeamish, '*oh-I-don't-really-wanna-be-here*'-rs.

The – '*I don't know, I've got a great girl at home ones*' – who try to relax by preferring to '*just have a chat*' and ask about your life story like it's as interesting as the ten girls who've gone before and then, just as your five minutes no-dancing time (breach of which incurs a fifty quid fine) is up, he drops his business card on the floor.

Nina   The table bends in the middle with the weight of the New Wave Heal's plates and my head aches with the boredom of their art dealing; prescription drug comparing; wannabe grown-up conversation.

They're all just as bored as me it seems, as I'm soon recruited in to tell stories of my 'exotic' life of oiled-up limbs and two-grand tips.

I got loads of them, so I begin …

'If ever there was such a thing as a wholesome stripper – she was it.

She had huge tits, which wobbled like peach jelly when she walked and hips that could sink ships with one swift wave of a sashay.

But instead, she used them as a mother would, bringing us Earl Grey tea on a polished silver tray, and we'd sip it in the changing room from cups that were made of such fine white china that the wilder girls would sometimes try and grind them into lines.

She was so kind, the kind of woman who offered us smiles and mints when hearts were sinking with the weight of rejection, who affectionately rallied us to count the joys of our job as we sobbed, wishing we'd been born boys.

We were never sure how she made any money, she was always so busy treating us to teatime breaks and honeydrop cakes and fending off the fakes

(those are the twats that didn't want to pay)

until one day I peeped into the private room, the one where no one except the wholesome one was allowed to go.

Peeping through a hole as small as a small toenail I spied puffed plush pillowed points of reference pointing in deference to the middle of the room.

And there, there were no poles.

Just a stripper shoe on the floor, high-rise plastic soles halfcovered in sand, a seaweed-stained hand caressing a greenish scaly tail.

I was trying to understand what was the hell was going on.

I felt a swell sail up, rise in my tassle-covered tummy and turned my head down and around.

I'd never been fond of the seaside, the thick smell of the sea floor had always made me feel unclean and a scar of sand would land me in the shower with a loofer for hours.

And now the scent of picked up pebbles and webbed feet permeated through the very door I stood at, though I was on dry ground.

Looked up again, rigid, ready, I couldn't quite believe what I'd found.

I saw her face. Full of flirty smiles and crafty glances down to her sequin-tipped tail which flick-flicked into the top of the top clients' drinks.

They were sinking into their chairs with looks of unchecked desire, loosening their silk ties, pulling their trousers up from the knee a little higher.

The wholesome stripper, the motherly figure full of tea and sweets who was before me now without any feet, was nearly swimming in red-hued notes as they floated down to the ground having been poked in awe into her shell-covered bra.

All this time of wondering when and how she worked, rumours asserting they'd seen her get cash for going down on the Filipino busboy with the strangely shaped tash.

But at least now I knew the truth.

The Effect by Lucy Prebble

I can tell the difference between who I am and a side effect.

The Effect was co-produced by Headlong and the National Theatre and received its world premiere at the National Theatre's Cottesloe Theatre on 6 November 2012. It was directed by Rupert Goold.

Context

Two pharmaceutical drugs trial volunteers, Tristan and Connie, consent to being given ever-larger doses of as-yet untested new drugs. Two doctors monitor the effect. The volunteers suffer from another even more potent reaction – love – but are not sure if it is real, or a toxic result of dopamine. The doctors argue about whether what has happened is chemically induced and therefore something that can be treated by other drugs, or something naturally real and unprompted. Technically, the playwright finds tidy symmetry between the lives of both the medical and volunteer couples. They seem, at points, to blur into a combined larger universal experiment that questions not only the efficacy of drugs and the pharmaceutical industry, but also identity, truth and the power and majesty of human love.

Acting notes

Dr James is used to the world of quantifiable data and the unquestionable order and precision that facts bring to her professional life. Her personal life is very different; it is a mess. When approaching this speech the actor must track down the clues that betray her subconscious or inner thinking, because although she reveals a lot about herself, there are very few stated reasons as to why her personal life has been so difficult. In describing her quest for companionship, on the transitory conference circuit, with all of its disastrous casual encounters, does this suggest that she has surrendered to the chancy, self-destructive desperate need of the lonely? If so, why offer this confession to Toby, her medical colleague, not least as he has confessed that he loves her?

Forty-seven years old

Dr James   I was having a tough time, quite a few years ago. I'd broken up from a long relationship I'd been in forever and that was a big decision and I'd lost a parent after a long … time. And I was supposed to be going away for work, a conference, but I didn't know if I could, I'm afraid of flying and I nearly didn't make it. But I did, and that week turned out to be one of the best weeks of my life. Professionally and just, in terms of … fun and new horizons. I met lots of interesting people and got very – you know it was good. And I got on very well with one guy there who was great and funny and a force of real joy in the room. Even though I was a mess – and well he was married – but it was one of those chance encounters that give you hope, because you think god, there are great people out there and they seem to think I'm great and … It felt like – beginnings, you know. So on the flight back I was sat next to another doctor, a woman, and she recognised me and we talked and she knew this guy and she said, oh you didn't sleep with him did you? And I say no why?! (*She indicates through mouthing it and physicality that actually she did.*) So apparently he really puts it around, he's this notorious shagabout on the conference circuit and younger, less astute girls would, you know. And it was strange because it wasn't till then – … As we flew back I sort of felt something dissolve, in the jet stream, like something got eroded down. And by the time I got back it was dark.

Exit by Steven Berkoff

Are you trying to tell me that all those hundreds of thousands of decent British men and women who peacefully marched in London to protest their right to hunt are all nutters ... Are you seriously saying that?

Exit was first published in *Steven Berkoff One-Act Plays* by Bloomsbury Methuen Drama in 2012.

Context

In this one-act play, we encounter a young couple who are having an everyday type of argument over nothing very much at all. Berkoff's finely-tuned, closely-observed language is at first playful with the two characters, Anne and Ben, trading insults in a familiar almost flirty and affectionate way. But in a matter of only a few lines, Berkoff skilfully changes the dynamic to that of all-out hostility. In Berkoff's hands, the argument becomes like a domestic war where we see both Anne and Ben engage in a quite torrid exchange of truths and half-truths, accusations and lies. The scene shifts from the cosy familiarity of bickering and banter to the last pathetic moments of what was once a loving relationship.

Acting notes

This is a heart-wrenchingly honest speech by a young woman who has realized that she has made the wrong choice. Her partner, Ben, is not the man she thought or hoped he would be. The speech comes in the last moments of the play, after all the shouting and screaming, all the insults and attacks have taken place. Anne is not a wronged woman or victim, and it is clear in the speech that she attains a state of painfully gained clarity and wisdom. She assesses her past with Ben and maps out her future, which she now realizes will most certainly be without him. The speech is economically written, with gaps and pauses between thoughts and words that remain incomplete. It is these moments in the speech where Anne's truth really lies. The performance depends not only on a clear and authentic connection to what is spoken but, crucially, the consideration of the very detailed inner life that, in the silences, clearly articulates the life she once had with Ben. In the silence, Anne imagines her new solitary life. Berkoff has literally hard-wired a sort of thinking-score and indicated very clearly where these inner moments overwhelm the spoken expression. To perform this, two separate thinking channels should be imagined running simultaneously; Anna's outer, spoken world, and the silent secret unspoken thoughts of a woman who has just broken away from all that is settled and sure. For Anna, the future is something formless, terrifying and new; we must experience her realization of this.

Young, alert, intelligent

Anne   At the beginning you try to make something work ... something come to life ... You try ... even if at the time I didn't really think or feel that we were suited to each other ... Something about coming home to a light on ... You imagine what it would be like ... There's always a time to dream ... *this* may work ... This time it could be good, since you hold the ideal up in front of your eyes ... like some pink cellophane ... enough of living alone ... I want to curl up to the same familiar smell ... to make a home ... That's what I wanted ... Something all humans want ... above anything ... that word, 'home', that's what I wanted ... to function as a woman ... to be loved and to give it ... Strong certain love ... I try ... I did ... but there is a time ... You get taken for granted ... used, too ... Then you hardly touch ... I become like your need ... your mother ... there to blow your nose ... keep you company ... because you can't face yourself ... It's terrible, and what's terrible is that because we both want that thing ... that elusive thing we don't admit that we might not just have it ... so ... maybe live and die alone ... you and your book of numbers ... anything to fill the space of an empty night ... doesn't matter who ... just fill them ... You men ... your kind of man is always alone ... aren't sure of who or what you are ... so we help you find yourself ... and become your mirror, but you can only see how glamorous you are ... how wonderful ... but eventually it all turns sour, the relationship becomes fake ... You just want someone to wipe your arse ... You use us like Kleenex ... So I will go ... I will ... to be alone may be the only way to truly find out who I am and who you are ... I can't comfort you, so don't run to me any more ... I'm going, so get used to it ... I will ... To fight is just another way to cover up the emptiness ...

Free Fall by Vinay Patel

Still, you'll get a real. Ice view of daybreak over the Estuary. All that smog really brings out the colours, y'know? Wouldn't think flying dirt could look that pretty.

Free Fall received its world premiere at the Pleasance Theatre, London on 14 October 2014, and was directed by Bethany Pitts.

Context

Half midnight at the Queen Elizabeth II Dartford Crossing. Andrea stands at the top of the Bridge, slowly gathering the courage to kill herself, whilst toll-booth worker Roland is settled in for yet another lonely night of supervising the toll-machines and hoping for someone, anyone, to talk to. Neither of them want to be there, but neither of them can free themselves from the hopeless messed-up lives they live. The play, set over the length of Roland's toll-booth late shift, is a bittersweet mix of poignant near-hopeless exchanges between two desperately lost souls that momentarily encounter a sort of accidental companionship. As the night slowly passes, Roland and Andrea find that they really do connect, in spite of their loneliness; is it the time of night, or unusual location, or is it that they have found the crossing to be a teetering place of hope?

Acting notes

Although the context of Andrea's speech is certainly quite bleak, her words are not the final desperate thoughts of someone who is going to end it all. The actor should be careful not to hold the speech in clichéd 'going to jump' style – all panicky and irrational. The speech is short and direct, betraying perhaps a newly-found confidence and surprising sense of purpose. She wants Roland to listen to her, she wants to explain how she feels and what she thinks. For Andrea, therapy and pills are something that she has 'done'; what she is now doing is actually communicating to someone who might understand or even care about her. The clarity of her thought is striking. She had been only moments away from jumping, but now realizes that her actual achievement may be that she is capable of making a decision – to either live or die. Such power is a new freedom yet to be fully experienced, but it brings a kind of joyous realization.

Early twenties – White, Essex

Andrea   No, listen! You need to fucking listen to me, Roland, listen to someone else for once, yeah? I'm not looking for your money, or your attention. I have just calmly accepted, like an adult, that I don't want to teeter along no more, hoping that it's all going to get better.

I've done the therapy, done the pills, done all of that inside, that didn't fuck me up, they tried to help. They try to get you to make little changes, little things to get you by. Routines. Tricks. But they aren't enough, it's too little paint over too many cracks. It's bigger than that, something big in here, something has gone totally wrong. No, was always wrong, and it's not the kinda thing that feels like you can get fixed.

He attempts to speak, but she cuts him off, while delicately placing a domino on the increasingly tall tower.

Andrea   Yeah, you get good days. Where everything is great. Where you want to live your life for other people, give them everything – stop being some mopey, selfish bitch. You even get it into your head that maybe there's a chance you can change, be alright, that you can solve everything before bedtime.

But you still wake up broken the next morning, and that's not living, that's coping, and, Mr Roland, I am so very, very tired of coping. It's the worst kind of existence.

But look, it's alright, all of that doesn't matter, yeah, 'cause here's the wonderful thing, the really most wonderful thing. When I made a decision, when I jumped. It was this incredible sensation ... It was bliss.

Hidden in the Sand by James Phillips

I think we've been waiting for each other
And so I'm going to trust you. That's all you can do with people.
Say this is my heart and if you drop it then it will break.

Hidden in the Sand received its world premiere on 1 October 2013 at the Trafalgar Studios, London. It was directed by the writer, James Phillips.

Context

A beautiful Greek Cypriot refugee, Alexandra, living in London and running a modest jewellery store, is seduced one night by middle-aged Jonathan, an awkward but charming English classical scholar. He studies an unknown classical past whereas she is trying to forget hers. Can such an accidental coupling result in more than just a clumsy one-night stand? Alexandra must confront the memories of her life before London, which are firmly locked away, stored like a painful set of secrets in a jewellery box. Jonathan, too, must learn to deal with the historical past in a new way if he is ever going to have a future with this beautiful, but troubled, woman. James Phillips' play is a haunting evocation of love at its most simple and true, but it is also a ghost story where the facts of the past have to be re-imagined and thought through anew. Its poetic, intimate, almost dreamy literary style is offset by an eerie, ever-present feeling that every encounter we have in life is totally out of our control. There are very different types of passion within the two selected speeches from this play. In terms of performance, neither should be acted with broad brush stroke emotion, but rather each one must be an understood experience, informed by very personal detail. Passion must be an impulse informed by something, not just itself.

Acting notes

In the first speech, Alexandra talks of a moment in the past that dramatically affected her entire life. Alexandra doesn't privilege us with too much detail, as if preserving it for herself alone. The repetition of 'He was' and 'He had', suggests that the man she describes was the centre of that moment but is now no longer part of her life. Why has this changed? James Phillips's evocative and mournful language offers the actor many images, which include Alexandra's own physical appearance and the forearms and silver watch-strap of the man she speaks of. These, if imaginatively connected to, authenticate the moment of thought by giving an essential thinking rhythm that is separate to the more obvious spoken rhythm. Not all words will imaginatively resonate within a speech, and the actor should be careful not to attempt an image-by-image translation, like a set of flicker cards prompting empty responses. But the text offers more than just text to speak; it should be able to generate a connected and vivid emotional life. In the second speech, Alexandra's niece, Sophia, describes the extraordinary moment when she had taken a photograph, only to find that she was accidentally documenting the brutality of a war-zone. Her matter of fact description, with all its many details of what camera lens and aperture were used, are rendered tragically insignificant by the memory she has of the sound of gun shot. Memory of events is always contextualized by one's emotional relationship to that event. What is Sophia's?

Alexandra   He was my best friend. No, it is –

He was the man I trusted best in the whole world.

He was older than me.

If someone is six years older then it takes twenty years to catch up. So he was always older. Even after we were lovers. Now we would be the same age. He was always older. He made decisions. He had travelled. We had never been anywhere.

He had those forearms that good men have, strong forearms. His watch had a silver strap. He wore denim shirts often. He never wore a tie, almost never. He was a journalist.

He was a writer, he was a wonderful writer. He let me read his poems, one day, when I was fourteen. He was going to write a great novel, about the Crusader Knights in Famagusta.

I met him first. On the beach at Salamis. I was eight years old, this awful little girl with hair tied up from her face, always asking people questions. I asked him questions. I used to plan them. I followed him around. He was so handsome. At first it was just me that knew him, was shadowing him, for many months, and then he met my family. I introduced him to them, on the veranda of the King George Hotel. I was sure then that one day he would be my husband. My sister Eleni and my parents sitting there looking up at him in the sunlight, he was my prize. He was fifteen years old.

Sophia   You see the black in the white of the clouds? The blur, those shapes?

Sophia   It is crows. For weeks before this I had been photographing crows. I seemed to see them wherever I went. I made them my personal project. (*Smiles.*) Strangely *The Sunday Times* are still refusing to print my seven pages on the crows of Yugoslavia.

When I took the shot I was looking at the crows not the men. I was tired. My best pictures all came when I was tired. We'd been travelling all day, because we heard a rumour about what was going on in this particular grisly area.

You can see the bowl of the valley and the sky because I used a 28mm lens. It's wider than the eye sees. I'd changed the lens when I saw the composition of the shot. And the clouds that people like, I put a yellow filter on the lens to bring out their drama, to bring out their contrast. The filter was in my bag. I took it out and screwed it on. Throughout all this preparatory work I knew in the back of my mind that a man was about to be killed. I was very quiet.

I slowed the shutter speed right down, 1/8 maybe, that's why the blur, that's why you see the motion of the gun. And of the crows. Why it became art. It was a conscious decision, pre-visualised, do you see Aunty-mou, everything was compositional. But it was the crows that drew me in. It was the motion of the crows that made me realise I had heard a gunshot. I had been counting under my breath, not for the execution, but for the position of the crows against the clouds. It was a landscape I was shooting, not a murder.

A History of Falling Things by James Graham

*I just. Wanted to tell stories. Loved them growing up. Even though
they generally scared the shit out of me. Think children's stories
can be the scariest of all.*

A History of Falling Things was first performed at Clwyd Theatre, Mold,
on 23 April 2009. It was directed by Kate Wasserberg.

Context

The play is a romantic almost sentimental comedy about fear, or more
precisely, irrational fear, including the fear of falling things: shoes, satellites, almost anything. Robin and Jacqui are virtually neighbours and
most significantly, virtual lovers, who only meet online because they
both posses such fears. In his introduction, playwright James Graham
describes how the play is 'essentially a relationship drama' and that 'many
of Robin's annoying, irrational anxieties' resemble his own. The play
is brilliantly crafted with dream-like sequences that are both funny and
achingly sad in the same moment. The fears are overwhelming and life
is clearly passing both Robin and Jacqui by as we see their bewildered
worlds diminish.

Acting notes

Like many of the characters in James Graham's plays, their ordinariness
should not be seen as being in any way simple. In *A History of Falling
Things*, the character Jacqui is seemingly just an average sort of girl who
had the misfortune of being in the wrong place at the wrong time. She
recounts the day that she had the bad luck to be on the 7/7 Underground
train in London when the bomb went off. We learn that she was on the
train, but not in the carriage that exploded, killing many passengers. Her
account of this has a dream-like quality, with a gradual description of
each moment, calmly removing it from reality. Her account of the bomb
blast is very moving, but more so is her need to justify how she has coped
since that terrible day. The actor must decide whether Jacqui has been
damaged by this moment or is merely reflecting upon it. Was the blueprint
for her character changed by this event or has she always been 'different
to everyone'?

Jacqui   I'd changed at Embankment and got on to the Circle Line. Never normally get a seat, that time of the day, Circle Line. But someone got off and I was the nearest so … and we were heading round to Liverpool Street. And just before we got to Aldgate, the train pulled to a halt. Nothing strange about that, always stopping. Stop, start, stop, start. Only it didn't move for, like, ten minutes. And people were grumbling and sighing. And then the lights went out.

And at first there was that titter of laughter, like 'What next?' And then more moaning. And then eventually there was just silence. And in the dark I started getting these flashes. Like flashes of being trapped. And the tunnels collapsing in. And rubble dropping down. And it felt like the oxygen was getting less and I felt like I was getting cramped and I started to begin panicking and then –

– we started reversing backwards. It was when we got out that we heard a bomb had gone off. Near Aldgate East. And three more around London . . .

Everyone one else … there was this sense of, like, 'defiance'. Or … of just not being afraid. And a unity in 'not being afraid', but the problem was I *was* afraid. Of something completely different, which made me feel different to everyone else. And the dreams at first were of ceilings and roofs, and then of … planes … and then of … well, you know what. And who knows why? Maybe because everything else felt irrational. Freak occurrences. And I know satellites must seem, to normal people, must seem irrational. Maybe I just needed something that was always up there. That could come down at any point. Just to justify the way I was feeling –

If You Don't Let Us Dream, We Won't Let You Sleep by Anders Lustgarten

*I don't know what you're afraid of but I know what it looks like. I
was married to fear most of my life
Don't give in to it.*

If You Don't Let Us Dream, We Won't Let You Sleep received its world
premiere at the Royal Court Theatre, London, on 15 February 2013. It was
directed by Simon Godwin.

Context

According to the playwright Anders Lustgarten, this satire was written
'for the return of political theatre' and to help people understand the
'killer zombie', also known as the 'market knows best' approach to
austerity. Lustgarten describes how people have been turned off politics
because they believe that it makes absolutely no difference. He sees this
play not as old-style agit-prop but 'anti-prop', populated with a vast range
of suited government officials, business representatives and politicos
working to targets and developing cost-effective plans that will remove
the current culture of the poor and give the investor a good return. We also
meet disaffected teachers, nurses and a group of dissidents who attempt
to establish a Court of Public Opinion in which the reasons and creators
of economic austerity will be put on trial. Lustgarten says the play was
written 'to make you feel and therefore to think'.

Acting notes

Playing any character who is essentially a political idea is difficult in
the context of a monologue or speech for audition because the performance can become overwhelmed by the logic of the argument and it can
therefore appear more like a spoken manifesto rather than a living voice
and presence. This has always been the challenge of political theatre from
George Bernard Shaw to Bertolt Brecht. This play's original setting was
without concrete location and was performed 'without décor'. A multitude
of interchangeable characters were, by their sheer critical mass, seemingly
anonymous, named only by their trade (workman, nurse, administrator)
and seemed to exist in the moment of an immediate idea as opposed to as

a sum of their lives. Therefore be cautious – to play a 'nurse' is to play nobody at all. People are not defined by generic labels but by their action or inaction.

Kelly is an idealist whose experience as an activist is so far limited, but she has many questions and hopes for change but she struggles to find a practical or workable way to achieve it. Her fears are that the country's current issues of unemployment, poverty and debt are trapped in theoretical rather than compassionate or active debate. Later in the play, she even describes how in Mesopotamia, three thousand years ago, they had a debt jubilee every seven years, where recorded debts were publicly smashed. So the challenge for the actor is how to play an educated idealist and not some cartoon cut-out student activist: to reveal her confusion and passion of thought, mixed with her intelligence and hopes for moral justice. Kelly unpacks a personal political theory to Tom, one that ostensibly shows her as a strong young woman of conviction and ethical principle. The skill for the actor is to understand that such an unpacking also makes her incredibly vulnerable; she exposes not only her political credentials, but also her private and personal ones too ('And love is the thing we're most frightened of'). What drives this confession? In this simple exchange of ideologies, Kelly reveals her innermost feelings. We experience the anger of the manifesto measured in human terms by a woman's doubts about the centralized global market place where the world's governments control everything, except perhaps the hearts and minds of the sceptical. Lustgarten's writing is so beautifully crafted that his blending of national themes with the personal does not compromise the very real experience of character we are presented with. The actor must summon the same skill, the same astonishing complexity in the formation of Kelly.

A political activist, late twenties-early thirties

Kelly All my mates ask me that. And when I tell them we don't have one, yet, they look all smug. Like I failed the test, so they're allowed to keep their shit facial hair and retro T-shirts and ironic hipster detachment that masks an abyss of emptiness. Like they don't have to think.

Tom (I'm not trying to be a dick. I just … I need this.)

Kelly Before I came here I was a student. Anthropology. In terms of making a living you'd be better off burning twenty grand's worth of scratchcards, but totally fascinating. One of the books we read was about debt. The writer was talking to this woman about the IMF and the horrible shit it gets up to, and after he laid out that people *die* in the name of austerity, have been doing in Africa for quite some time, she just looked at him and said: 'But they have debts. They have to pay them.' And he was amazed by this, that debt has such a powerful hold on us that a perfectly reasonable woman can think it's better for people to die than for financial imbalances to be corrected. And he started to dig into why. And he concludes, five hundred pages later, that it's because our deepest social ties and obligations – to our ancestors, to the society that birthed us – we express in terms of debts. That at its deepest level, debt is our word for love.

Tom (Hah. That's quite … I never thought of it like that.)

Kelly Debt is our word for love. And love is the thing we're most frightened of. And you can't take on a deep, atavistic, millennia-old thing like that without a new space and a new language. It's not the answers right now, it's the questions. We are trying to learn to ask the right questions, ones that don't start with money, that start with people. Asking those questions: that's the alternative, Tom.

Josephine and I by Cush Jumbo

I wanted to change. I've always wanted to change but you cannot achieve that without power. We cannot find equality stuck at the bottom of the bottom of the bottom.

Josephine and I received its world premiere at the Bush Theatre, London, on Friday 12 July 2013 in a production directed by Phyllida Lloyd.

Context

Josephine and I is a solo play set in a cabaret-style nightclub where a pianist plays show-tunes, and the audience sits very close to the performance area. The play seamlessly intertwines two stories: one about the great yet almost forgotten jazz entertainer Josephine Baker, and the other about the more modest life of an aspiring young, struggling actress. Along the way we meet a host of extraordinary characters from both their lives, including a Tiny Tears dolly with gaudy Josephine Baker makeover, and, in the original production at least, the performer's little dog. The play is an exhilarating mix of jazz-age reportage and personal anecdote. As the two stories increasingly become one, with both women experiencing similar forms of prejudice many decades apart. The play ends with a sort of solo duet as the performer sings Bob Dylan's, *The Times They Are a-Changin'*. The story told at this moment could be either the actress or Josephine.

Acting notes

In this speech, the linguistic quality has a very 'real' conversational feel. The performance style should be as natural as possible. Actors generally associate the word 'style' with something other than natural, as though it equates to performed heightened extremes that are in some way removed from the real. Stanislavski has shown that 'real' and 'natural' modes of performance need to be prepared and are not achievable by ill-considered guesswork. *Josephine and I* has the candid, open-hearted, off-the-cuff honest appeal of listening to a best friend chatting intimately about her life. The girl in this speech reveals so many things about her relationship with her boyfriend, his need to settle down and have children, and her own desire to remain relatively free and childless, or at least until she has done everything that she needs to do in her life. Ideas and thoughts just spill out of her excited and rushing mind. Why does she feel that she hasn't achieved very much when she is still so young? What does this say about her background? Is she putting on a brave face or does she really possess the incredible optimism that she seems to display? There is something almost conspiratorial in the way that she describes her boyfriend, as if by telling us about him, we too will understand why she might want to leave him. The speech could be delivered in a delightfully bright tone but on closer examination we see that she frequently uses negatives as opposed to positives when describing her situation. This fusion of seemingly light-spirited ease with her darker, more anxious confessional manner, is particularly challenging to achieve in performance, for both aspects of her life will need to be signalled if the speech is to be fully realized.

Late twenties

Girl   It's hilarious! My boyfriend David wants marriage and kids. He is absolutely definite about it. Usually men in their thirties can't even hear the word 'pregnancy' without putting their hands over their ears and bursting into tears. But David says there's nothing in the world he wants more than to have a family with me. Even more than he wants an end to greenhouse gases. It's lovely. *But*, when he first mentioned it to me we'd only been going out for about six months so I just laughed it off. Not because I don't want children but because I thought he was living in a bit of a dreamland. An environmental activist and an actress starting a family? It's not exactly the most financially stable situation, is it? They can't live on Shakespeare and compost. I just thought of that. In response to my laughter, David then came out with all the things people usually say about having children: 'There's *never* a right time. They're *not* as expensive as you think. All they *need* is love.' I love David but he has a way looking of at things that although it is beautifully positive is completely unrealistic. Having a child is like having the most physically and emotionally hungry pedigree tiger. You can't just feed it frozen pizza, give it a hug now and then and hope for the best. I mean, bring it up wrong and it could kill someone. And what about the time? I mean, I don't know how other actors have children. They're heroes. There isn't enough room in my brain for that audition, that job, those lines, my family, my boyfriend, my dog *and* a baby. Nor should there need to be. A child deserves more, surely? David has this passion for making the world a better place, I mean, who wouldn't want him as a husband and father? I've never met a man who I've so badly wanted to get stretch marks for but obviously not right now. Not until I've done everything I *need* to do.

The Kindness of Strangers by Curious Directive

You never forget your first shift. Sheets of snow. In April. 1985.
My son had just been born. I had to try to save a baby just a few
months older than him on my first trip out. Nightmare.

The Kindness of Strangers was a co-production between Curious Directive
and the Norfolk & Norwich Festival. It was first performed in May 2013
and toured the UK in 2014. It was directed by Jack Lowe.

Context

The Kindness of Strangers began life in the back of an ambulance. In
director Jack Lowe's introduction to the play, he describes how his mother
told him a story about paramedics travelling from Norwich to London.
His research, with the company Curious Directive, led him to have many
conversations with ambulance staff and those working in the NHS. The
result was not translated into a heart-rending stage play, but a site-specific
ushering of the audience into 'Old Rosie', a 1968 ambulance, and an
encounter with the voices and lives of the paramedic world. Five audience
members at a time, each wearing earphones, embark on an average night's
work on the front line. We meet Sylvia on her last shift and Lisa on her
first. While on the imagined journey, the ambulance doors are flung open,
onto different emergency scenarios.

Acting notes

In a touching story, Lisa explains to her fellow worker, Sylvia, why she became
a paramedic. As she remembers the event, the emotional speech is both
difficult and personal. The telling of it triggers Lisa's childhood memories of
that time, and the decision she made, after having a bad fall from a tree, to be
like the paramedics who rescued her. There is something spellbinding about
her simple little story, and the matter-of-fact acceptance of what she would
one day become. It might be tempting to demonstrate lots of emotional range
but Lisa's story is so ordinary and, although the memory of that time is vivid
and real, her words are not dramatic or heroic. The real emotion is focused on
the person she is telling the story to, for she is angry with her colleague, and
her anger accidentally reveals this personal moment. What is it that she sees
in her colleague that she associates with that time?

Paramedic. Mid-thirties

Lisa   How can you be so compassionate, so warm and loving to people you've never met and *so shitty to me*.

You know why I'm here? Why I went through the hours of exams, weight training, was asked questions I wouldn't wish on my worst enemy and stayed up until 3am, yeah, until about *now* every night working in a bar to pay for my training?

I was seven years old. Seven. And I'm up an elm tree in my gran's garden.

Winter time. I can remember it so clearly because school had finished and mum drove me down the M4 to London to stay with gran. I burst into tears because I was worried mum wouldn't take me home again. It was nearly Christmas.

My gran told me, 'You can crawl through the bushes in the garden but don't climb upwards'.

And of course as soon as gran was out shopping, granddad gave me a wink and up I went, peering over the fence into the neighbours' garden.

The neighbours came out of their backdoor with their dog. I slipped.

The thump on the ground was the first time I'd ever been winded. I thought I was dying. That and the fact my radius had burst through my skin and was just stuck there under my jumper. That's why my arm's like an oxbow lake now.

I didn't really say anything. I just cried and cried and cried and cried but then I remember seeing these two green figures out of the corner of my eye, bounding towards me.

They didn't move me to begin with but started talking about *The Transformers*, which I thought was amazing. Asking me questions like which was my favourite? Optimus Prime – obviously. Then they asked whether I'd seen Aladdin. One of them started doing an impression of Abu, bouncing around the garden with a canulation kit … And my crying turned to laughing, laughing so hard I was crying.

And this all came from a *Transformers* logo on my jumper and a VHS they'd seen on the sitting room floor as they rushed through the bay windows, down the patio steps and out to me.

We sat in the ambulance, going maybe seventy miles an hour. They raced up the high street and picked up Gran from Sainsbury's and we all sat in the ambulance singing, 'Arabian Nights' at the top of our voices and telling 'Knock Knock' jokes. It. Was. Brilliant.

They made me feel on top of the world in the exact moment where I should've, on every level, felt like it was on top of me.

My arm was severely broken, I'd betrayed my gran, my granddad was in trouble for letting me climb a tree and I was missing *Rugrats*. My laughter released so many endorphins I still get a tingle up my spine when I think about it.

Mcqueen, or Lee and Beauty by James Phillips

*You look otherworldly. Like all my girls. This will make you a
queen. Like years ago and people wore clothes like weapons, like
weapons against poor people, because even if you were hungry,
how could you raise your fist against what looked like a god?*

McQueen, or Lee and Beauty received its world premiere at St James
Theatre, London, on 12 May 2015. It was directed by John Caird.

Context

The story takes place in London over a single night. James Philips
suggests that 'it is inspired by a love of the talent of the designer Alexander
McQueen. It is not a documentary, nor biography. It is a fairy story, like
a McQueen show.' The play opens in the relative calm of McQueen's
huge 'shambolic basement' in Mayfair, with its mannequins, clothes and
chaos. A woman appears through the debris, the basement is under attack
– or investigation, visited as it is by an apparition or most certainly, an
uninvited guest. Dahlia, an adoring fan wants a dress. McQueen inter-
rogates her – 'You broke into my house', he exclaims; 'the door was
open', she replies. And so this dream-like ghostly homage to the world
of this famous designer begins. Both take a journey through London, and
the fairy-story landscape of one of the world's greatest contemporary
artists. Dahlia, we learn, is his alter-ego, and in a sequence of beautifully
haunting encounters, almost reminiscent of Scrooge's midnight trip to
salvation, we cross to the East End of London of his past, and meet the
tailors where he worked as a cutter, the fashion stylist Isabella Blow, and
see 'the precious finger nails broken, hanging, poised between inspiration
and inactivity, listening for that second beat of your heart'. The journey
fuels Dahlia's growing depression and doubt, McQueen's success being
like an uncontrollable storm 'like when you're lost in snow or something'.
This is a play for the imagination.

Acting Notes

In this scene, 'The girl who watched from a tree', Dahlia is essentially
McQueen. That is certainly an acting challenge. She is his inner thought
and reflection, but in the speech it is as if he hasn't acknowledged this.

Dahlia's growing sense of placement and connection, her realization that 'we were twins', requires clear motivational reasoning, or it will just float away or become merely the speech of a phantom stalker fan. The performer has to therefore embody McQueen's doubt about his life and career, and allow his thinking rhythm to reside in her body. We are all capable of inhabiting the imagined momentary thoughts of others, but the performer must use Dahlia as a vehicle for discovery. Why would the character choose this other persona to learn about himself? The mix of personalities, genders and states of being makes this speech a wonderfully creative challenge. How to play a ghost woman, whilst at the same time be a man?

Dahlia   I wasn't up there all the time. I'm very clean. I had comfort breaks and everything. I was watching for a way in at first. And then I saw you. Or not saw you, not really, just became aware that there was someone in the house. Just like a shadow in the house. You're so quiet aren't you? Not out all the time, not loud, a good man. Just the little television in the corner of one room. And so I suddenly wondered whether you just work all the time, all day and night. Or just sat there thinking. You make these things, these things that people love. I looked you up online. I looked at all the pictures. People have opinions about you. They write essays and stuff.

I have been very lonely recently and I don't sleep well so it was easy to watch. I don't like going out any more but also I don't like being alone. Are you like that?

You don't sleep much either, do you? We were awake the same times, like we were twins I thought.

Tonight I knew you were still away. I liked watching the house for you. People who can't sleep should be protected. But I wanted my dress very badly tonight and I felt like I couldn't get through to dawn without it. And so I came down from the tree and I walked as quietly as I could down the length of the yard, walking like I was invisible like when you're a really small kid and you close your eyes so nobody can see you. And I thought I'd have to smash something to get in, I picked up a stone to smash something, but then when I got to the door I just knew it would be open, I knew it was left open and I put my hand on it and it was, and the house it was welcoming me in –

Morning by Simon Stephens

Don't think you've stopped me leaving because you haven't

Morning received its world premiere at the Traverse Theatre, Edinburgh, in a production by the Lyric Hammersmith on 1 August 2012. It was directed by Sean Holmes.

Context

Teenagers Stephanie, whose Mum is dying, and best friend Cat, who is going to college, suggest to their young friend Stephen that a threesome might be fun. Though very surprised at their suggestion, he thinks that it might be a good idea too. The event quickly turns from being awkward teenage fumblings to something very different when they start biting him and pulling his hair. Stephen is eventually tied-up and Stephanie kills him with a rock. Not out of anger or self-defence but, it would seem, just for something to do. This moment is so shocking and surprising. It is the complete randomness of the action and subsequent dead-eyed negation of responsibility or remorse that is so disturbing. Stephanie admits to Cat that she knows what she has done but is not affected by it. She is just a kid.

Acting notes

Stephanie's speech is so dark and uncompromising, its momentum driven by her utter despair. To perform such words will require not only quite extraordinary vocal strength, articulation and phrasing, but also a clear psychological map. If the words are just screamed out, as an anonymous angry tirade, the speech will lack crucial detail, and assume a generic or vague mood of anger or pain. This is the longest and only speech in the play and is spoken in isolation, as if directly to us. Is this an explanation or justification for her violence?

Seventeen

Stephanie   All music is shit and all art is shit and all theatre is shit and all television is shit and all sport is shit and all cinema is shit. The food is shit and everything is fucking shit. The streets and the furniture and computers and everybody is just stuck inside a vacuous vapid hole of just fear and horror and nasty fucking rancid vile shit. And there is no connection with anything and there is no future and all of the city is full of shit and there is waste everywhere and if I could I'd take all the waste that's gathered in the cities and put it into landfills and pour it out into the streets so that people can know what they have wasted every day and see the hundred million tons of shit every year put into the ground. You could make mountains of shit. You could sculpt the Alps out of shit. You could poison the seas with shit. And everybody wants a hopeful ending and there won't be one. We have a decade. And then everything will retract. Everybody wants a message and there is none. Everybody wants hope shining through the darkness and there isn't any. And we could take to the streets but it won't change anything. We could form a protest movement and it won't change anything. We could stand on the streets and give out flyers and it won't change anything. We could refuse to vote in the next election. We could all of us vote in the next election. We could burn down polling booths in the next election. We could smash in shop windows. We could repair all the shop windows. We could set fire to cars. We could repair all of the burned-out cars. We could recycle. We could refuse to recycle. None of it will change anything. There is only terror. There is no hope.

Playing with Grown-ups by Hannah Patterson

That's the problem isn't it?
Now we can have it all,
We're expected to bloody do it all.

Playing with Grown-ups was first performed at Theatre503, London, on 14 May 2013, directed by Hannah Eidinow.

Context

New mother, Joanna, is faced with what has recently become the dreary reality of endless sleepless nights filled with nappy-changing and the double exhaustion of a now near-loveless relationship. This wasn't part of the master plan. To make matters even worse, her ex-lover's unexpected visit, with his new very young girlfriend, Stella, doesn't help matters either. Carefree Stella is everything that Joanna once was but now despises. *Playing with Grown-ups* journeys between the extreme emotions of new parenthood – the delight and despair. With the baby now making three in the relationship, can Joanna and husband Robert really have it all?

Acting notes

Stella is sixteen years old; her boyfriend is hardly a boy at all but approaching early middle-age. Why would he want to take her to visit his middle-aged ex-girlfriend Joanna? Is the visit as innocent as it seems or is he showing her off as some sort of teenage trophy? In this speech, Stella states that she finds adults fascinating, which implies that she doesn't really consider herself to be one. Watching them as if they are animals at a zoo is not the same as being one. Is Stella's visit to Joanna part of this adult study or is she really just uncoupling herself from any respon- sibility, because, as a child, she doesn't really know how to be grown up? It is significant that Stella finds everything 'so simple', because the adult world that she experiences in Joanna and Robert's life, that of new parenthood and a fatigued relationship, is anything but simple. Is this a cool new philosophy or simply teenage naïvety? Her aversion to anything complicated would suggest that she is actually aware of how unusual her life is and is trying to block out further complications. In acting terms, Stella's complex life must not be reduced to that of a brat cliché. Something compels her to join adult company as an equal but also remain a kid. The inner world of such contradictions will be the rich technical scaffolding upon which any of Stella's outer characteristics must be built.

Sixteen years old

Stella   I find adults fascinating. I could watch them, for hours.
Much more than animals at the zoo. They make everything in life so
complicated. Then they say, 'Uh, if only everything in life wasn't so
complicated.' But I swear they enjoy it. They create it.

Beat.

To me it all seems so simple. If you like someone, tell them. If someone
is hurt, then help them. Sort out the problem, at the root. Don't just
patch it up, or ignore it. It'll only come back, and it'll hurt more the next
time.

Beat.

My mum always says to me, 'You don't understand because you haven't
experienced it yet. Once you experience it, then you'll know. Then
you'll feel it. Then you'll be able to empathise. Life is complicated.'
She talks as if I were an innocent. A blank canvas, fresh and ready for
the painting. But I'm not. She's the one that's forgotten. We aren't born
innocent. We're just born more obvious, that's all. With all our needs
and desires right out there in front of us, naked, for everyone to see. And
then we learn to hide them. Call them by different names. Make them
seem more sophisticated. To complicate it.

Beat.

Don't we?

Beat.

Well, that's how I see it.

Quiz Show by Rob Drummond

Ladies and gentlemen, boys and girls…

Quiz Show was first performed at the Traverse Theatre, Edinburgh, on 29 March 2013 by the Traverse Theatre Company and was directed by Hamish Pirie.

Context

Rob Drummond dramatically captures a sort of terrifying nostalgia for those now-lost family nights of our childhood, where we would sit around the telly with our families on a Saturday evening, watching tired-format, light-entertainment game shows, with all their odd contestants, meagre cash prizes and easy glamour. Every show had an unforgettable quiz master, and in Drummond's play Mr Daniel Caplin hosts a show called 'False', where 'there are no questions, only statements; where every one of those statements is a lie and where the prize is nothing less than the truth'. But all the razzmatazz of this particular quiz show offers not prizes, but trauma. The play's original staging cleverly engaged its spectators in a sort of 'studio audience' cliché of cheers, screams and applause, only to very theatrically implicate them later in much darker scenes at the end of the play.

Acting notes

Sandra is one of the 'False' game show contestants and proudly demonstrates her knowledge and expertise in the opening lines of this speech. Not just knowledge but also tactics, for she knows when to be 'false' and when to be true. But the fact that she struggles with most, is that the game show host sexually abused her. The speech is confessional in tone, almost like a statement. Her matter-of-factness is quite alarming: 'I was nice to him. I knew what he meant.' The performance challenge is to map out the growing memory of this terrible moment. Notice that the speech collapses linguistically, with longer, more fully-formed sentences at the start of it, and much shorter statements of fact at the end. Though virtually unspoken, the actual true memory takes possession in these moments. For the actor, the word is the last moment of thought.

Sandra (*down camera*)   Think of an experience from your childhood. Something you remember clearly, something you can see, feel, maybe even smell, as if you were really there. After all, you really were there at the time, weren't you? How else would you remember it? But here is the bombshell. You weren't there. Not a single atom that is in your body today was in your body when that event took place. Matter flows from place to place and momentarily comes together to be you. Whatever you are therefore, you are not the stuff of which you are made. If that doesn't make the hairs on the back of your neck stand up, you weren't listening properly.

I wrote that.

False. It was a scientist called Steve Grand.

When we experience something a sequence of neurons fire in the brain. And when we remember it the same sequence of neurons fires again. We are nothing but our memories. Good and bad. That is what we are made of.

I won the show, you know. I did. And not with a gun. Fair and square. With my mind. I won. I got to go through the door.

The prize was a video recorder.

After the show had gone off air, Gerry Holland said that Daniel Caplin wanted to hang out with me. I was excited. Gerry Holland delivered me personally to Daniel's dressing room while my parents waited for me in the green room.

Daniel was sitting on a writing desk. There was one of those things for putting pens in. And there was a Christmas tree in the corner. The whole place stank of pine. Daniel said he liked to keep a tree all year round. I thought that was odd. I remember thinking that was odd.

He said I was quite a nubile young lady. He said it quickly. Testing the water. He asked me if I knew what that meant. Of course I did. I'm the champion.

Daniel asked if I wanted to come on the show again next week. I said of course I did. I'm the champion.

He said there was a price I had to pay. Said I could only come back on if I was nice to him.

If I was nice to him.

I knew what he meant.

Red Velvet by Lolita Chakrabarti

It's like being at a crossroads – a point of absolute, unequivocal change. It makes my blood rush.

Red Velvet received its world premiere at the Tricycle Theatre, London, on 11 October 2102. It was directed Indhu Rubasingham.

Context

Lolita Chakrabarti's play is a true story about a young African-American actor called Ira Aldridge, who, when the great London stage actor Edmund Kean collapses on stage at the Theatre Royal, Covent Garden in 1833, is asked to take over the playing of the coveted role, Othello. It is also a play about racism, for Aldridge's performance caused such an outcry that it leads to the theatre's ultimate closure.

Acting notes

In this speech, Halina, a hopeful young journalist in search of an interview, is in the great theatre star's dressing room. She is clearly worried that he will call for the theatre manager and get her thrown out. This would be a disaster, so in a desperate attempt to stay, she explains how, after much planning, including bribing a stage hand, she gained access. As she speaks, she tries to find the right moment to explain her reasons for doing this, and while the audience hears her account, they also see Aldridge preparing to go on stage. He applies white stage make-up to his black skin. Chakrabarti brilliantly crafts this deeply poignant stage moment, exposing the racism of the age and Aldridge's necessary acceptance of it, without any comment or rage. What is so extraordinary is that she, in effect, gives Aldridge's speech away; for in dramatic terms at least, this would be the perfect scene for him to speak out, full-throated, against his unjust treatment. In so doing, the audience is confronted by the full emotional impact of this moment. Halina explains what she has done and begs for his forgiveness: she is poor and her father is very ill, or at least this is the reason she gives. Aldridge listens whilst he continues to apply the white paint. The challenge for the actor is to shape the emotional complexity of this moment. Halina knows that she has done wrong, but who wouldn't do the same in the circumstances? She also senses that

Aldridge may not be easily won over by her sob story or her profession as a journalist. The speech will require the performer to really conjure up Aldridge's great presence and silence. It is his silence that she responds to. In needing his story, the actor must reveal Halina's.

Halina   Is all men, the whole office. I am only woman you see. So everything I do is … is …

Ira   … (visible.)

Halina   Visible, yes. There's only one, how you call … water klosette … in the office right? And that's become huge trouble. I almost cause walk out strike. There are meetings, voting, new written rules. It was like awful. Now I have to ask one of them to check klosette and he puts a … er … a sign on the door when I'm in there. They all complaining. I say they should ring bell so whole district know my business.

Ira, now white faced, takes an oil stick and starts to draw in the lines of age – under the eyes, around the mouth at the temples. He glances at her with interest.

Halina   Sorry, it makes me … so … because … well, I don't mean to be boasting but … I'm so competent. I am. I speak German, Russian, Polish, English. My father says patience and he should know, he's not well. He worked for Mr Sheibler, your friend. A good man, I think, but America fighting, everybody wanting cotton, so Father worked too much, and dust from the cotton … he can't breathe good now, can't go out so … he knows patience believe me … We live near station and sometimes when trains come in, I wait for whistle and scream so loud. No one hears me. I sound crazy?

Ira   (Uhuh.)

Halina   Anyway I'm sorry. Father says I talk too much, that I should get to a point because after all that's reason for talking. When they said you were coming, there was such excitement … Father … he talk of your performance like it's yesterday … but it's nine years past! This is page two maybe even page one! …

He takes a long white hairpiece and puts it on and then attaches a thin white beard.

Halina   No one could place interview with you so I lie, said Father knew you and the boss, he said yes … I did total homework, read all articles, memoirs. I was too prepared really but … if I am not practising how will I learn? When you cancel … it's my only chance … so I made friend of Casimir … the stagehand … I promised … a … a date if I see your room.

Ira is ready. He is unsure what to do next.

Halina   I lie to get in here. I'm so sorry. I didn't mean … Really. I embarrass myself and forgot manners … please don't think me bad

... I'll lose my job. Please ... don't make complaint. I need to buy medicine. If I lose ... my father he ... I can't afford to ... I'm sorry. Really sorry.

A knock at the door.

Skin Tight by Gary Henderson

I wanted to see if I could live for just one second without thinking about you. I wanted to know that I could survive. That I could forget you if I had to. I wanted to kill you so they couldn't take you away from me.

Skin Tight had its world premiere at BATS Theatre, Wellington, New Zealand, in 1994. It was produced by Epsilon Productions on 16 July 2013 at the Park Theatre, London, and directed by Jemma Gross.

Context

Elizabeth and Tom are poetic lovers whose passion is vividly dramatized by Gary Henderson. Their romance is presented through a sequence of very physical exchanges, sometimes sensual, sometimes violent. What is certain is that they are irretrievably in love. *Skin Tight* charts their lives in an extraordinary non-linear way, with significant moments in their relationship dissolving with film-like fluidity into both past and present. Inspired by New Zealand poet Denis Glover's poem, *The Magpies,* we encounter a curious dream-like dance of lives at war and in love.

Acting notes

This is a particularly emotive speech, seemingly nostalgic in tone, but is in fact the voice of one who has experienced the trauma of war and loss. Elizabeth recounts the long unbearable weeks when her lover was a soldier away from home; she remembers the news of injured or lost men, and her lover's long-awaited return. Although the speech is rich in both language and imagery, the actual performance should not be about lines being delivered in a beautiful or poetic manner, but rather, the world of character, and in particular, Elizabeth's extraordinary capacity to cope with her fears of the unknown and her ability to deal with the horror of her lover's return. Speeches about the majesty of love so often wrong-foot the performer, as though love is all open vowel sounds and soft speaking. In this speech, the harsh realities of love and devotion are revealed in all their complexity. Is this the first time Elizabeth has found the need to reveal her truth or is it an oft-told story that brings with the telling of it some form of comfort for something that may now have been lost?

Elizabeth   And Lofty Allen with his big bony wrists sticking out the sleeves of his tunic. Like a boy with man's arms. And you. All of you. All our beautiful, indestructible boys, laughing in the sunlight. And we were utterly deceived, cheering and waving and weeping as the train pulled out. Except Mrs Heremaia. Back against the station wall in the shadows. Face like a rock. She knew. But the rest of us – the sunlight on Orari Station deceived us all.

And the telegrams started to come before you'd even had time to get over there. Every day someone else took it like a punch. Mrs Heremaia got hers. One for each son. Dear God, you'd think they could have left her one. Irene Woodhurst walking around for days, dry-eyed and stunned, then finally bursting into tears in Morrisons'. Howling. Embarrassing everybody. Calling Brian's name over and over. And the man behind the counter called her hysterical. She wasn't hysterical. Just … cheated.

Then you all started coming home. One by one. Gordon Douglas with no legs. Then Lofty Allen with a hollow in the side of his head where they'd put a metal plate. One by one.

And finally you.

She turns and puts her arms around him, laying her head against his back.

Standing in the sunlight on Orari Station. Looking as strong and perfect as I'd remembered you. I was afraid to believe it. You looked at me and held out your arms and said, 'Elizabeth'. And I ran to you, and it was the first time I'd seen you cry. And I, deceived again, thought the horror was finally over.

Because each night you told me something new. Every night some wound tore open inside you and a wave of blood washed out, drenching us in our bed. And inside each wound was another, deeper one. Macky Heremaia's head splattered across your tunic. Brian Woodhurst going under the tracks of a tank.

He turns and lays his head in her lap, curling up like a child.

You lay in my arms and wept and shook so badly I thought you were dying. I was afraid of sleeping; afraid of the nightmares. I was afraid of you.

Underneath by Pat Kinevane

Sticks and stones didn't break her bones
but words and pointing crushed her.
is beauty only really skin deep?
does ugliness hide somewhere deeper?

Underneath received its world premiere at the Lime Tree Theatre, Limerick, on 5 December 2014. It was directed by Jim Culleton.

Context

The play's original director, Jim Culleton explains that 'Pat wanted to write a play about a woman from Cobh whose name we do not know, and whose life had been shaped by the disfigurement she received when she was struck by lightning as a girl'. The play explores earthly prejudice, and unearthly beauty and how we treat people according to their appearance. The solo performer, 'Her', is required to 'conjure' every role in a space 'scattered' with a golden magazine, a golden lampshade, a golden wallpaper roll, a golden tea towel, a golden glove and two golden J-cloths. She speaks, disfigured by a lightning bolt, as if from the intimacy of the grave, her final resting place which could be Co. Cork or ancient Egypt for all of its gold domesticity. She was bullied, betrayed and burnt by life, and now in death's reflection is angry and yet philosophical.

Girls cleaned my face with red poppy soap and washed and dried
my hair.

Acting notes

The task for the performer playing this extraordinary speech is to identify a simple route through her reasoning. Why does *Downton Abbey* matter? Why would dwelling on the characters in this programme so annoy and upset her? Work out what is hidden in such seemingly humorous ranting. What is she searching for? Why will she not confront her anger with more obvious reflection? Is such avoidance due to the painful truth that she holds within her distraught understanding of her own life and death? Her jump in emotional tone and content from 'the day to day problems of the mega wealthy' to her melancholic memory of the picture of an

Egyptian queen, chocolate boxes and biscuit tins, requires a beautifully layered emotional state that both cherishes and despises what has gone before, whilst also accepting the impossible pointlessness of the present. Not the mad rambling of a disfigured woman – but the celestial clarity of an angel who knows.

The acting challenge in the second speech is quite clear. Such storytelling certainly requires a performance style that doesn't inadvertently collapse into the easy cliché of lyrical 'mad woman'. The writing is utterly incredible here – 'But I have seen how human beauty works' – and the trap for any performer at such moments of painful recognition is not to play character with single focus or such straight- lined easy inner-life. Such realizations are the result of life-felt pain and loss, fear, doubt, and even hopelessness. What are the stories that she hasn't told or the thoughts that have not been expressed? What drives these revelations? A strong dynamic inner-world will need to be constructed.

Her   And Downton fuckin' Abbey! Who gives a shit about the
day-to-day problems of the megawealthy in their humongous house?
Why does this fascinate people? Frocks galore with their spinach moose
and in this week's episode … the son and heir of everything ponders:
'Dear sweet one, shall I go to war, and miss your kiss, or ought I remain
here, and sip your piss! Carson, pour the wine. I feel an alteration. A
flux. Everything is changing, at Downton.' Who gives a shit? And as for
the servants downstairs complainin' … 'By gum, my hands is down to
the bone from all that scrubbin' – every time a bell rings Daisy's got to
doo things' – get over it! You're a servant, serve! Isn't it wonderful how
they all respect each other upstairs and down. Isn't it – how they tolerate
each other. It is amazing how we can re-write history, cos if you were
a servant back then, and you stepped out of line, they would kick the
living shit out of ya!

But I did answer Jasper. The only time I felt anywhere close to the land
of pretty was when I was eight. There was a dune of rubbish outside
the convent … an old sister had died and they were cleaning out her
cell. Big pile of empty chocolate boxes and biscuit tins … Big fat dead
nun! I saw this blackand-white picture, about this size which turned out
to be the lid of a jigsaw box. Two thousand pieces … The image was
faded. But the woman on the cover fascinated me. I took it to teacher.
She explained that the woman was an Egyptian Queen … Her name
was Nefertiti, meaning 'the perfect one has arrived'. Graceful neck,
impeccable visage. So, I had an idea. I would repair the royal lady and
make a present for mammy. She was gonna be twenty-five in May. I
drew over the outlines of her features to bring her back to life. I then
made a collage with remnants of yellow velvets and duck-egg silk …
but I didn't have any gold fabric. Mam always said it was bad luck to
wear gold … so I used Cadbury's foil instead, the bullion wrapper from
Tiffin and whole-nut bars. I felt like Big Fat Dead Nun … sneaking
around for weeks secretly munching.

Her   I know we need beauty, all of us. Need the glimpse of an exquisite landscape or Venus shimmering in the palm of the Moon. But I have seen how human beauty works. How the surface is rewarded above skill. How we flock to be around the beautiful ones and go out of our way to help them, how they get promoted faster and forgiven sooner. How some use it to get exactly what they desire crushing everybody in their paths. So when was the last time you judged another ... just because of this?

Third soul-sucking moment.

For my forty-eighth birthday, twelfth of the third, 'thirteen. The girls took me clubbing. The best night of my life. The last night of my life. They teased me to the floor after a couple of Smirnoffs! All I could see were shapes of others, their whitest eyes and grills of teeth.

Lights flashing. Dancing like the girl I always wanted to be ... soft at the shoulder and hip ... elegant and free on the waves of sound ... rolling on to glassy sand, sinking in the warm grains and the entire surface of me covered in tiny jewels, with no stammer, no temper, no disfigurement, no loneliness, nothing ... just jewels, dancing.

Her dancing ... and this ends ...

Next day, I was a factory. Made new curtains and bought a bag of paste, a brush and a lovely simple wallpaper to spruce up the chimney breast for Easter. Raggy ould clothes. The evening was still dull for March. Had the telly volume mute and glanced over now and then to see if there was any news from Rome of the new Papa. Very loud music upstairs from the girls as they were starting early, fair dues to them. I ran my cold tap to mix the paste in the basin. Wooden spoon. Then bell in hall went. I knew the girls wouldn't hear it so I buzzed the customer in. Routine. More mixing. Swirls. Knock on my door! Wrong one I'd explain. Tap off. Man outside coughing. 'Two seconds!' Whuu, heavy cologne. Open door.

Him. We don't see him ...

Well, the Perfect One arrives. What are the chances?! There it is again! – that look of disgust at me. Is it because I drew attention away from ya? Or were ya afraid that I was contagious? And that you'd itch, and scab, and peel, and we'd all see that your father is inside ya. Is there a Mrs Wade? Does she know you're paying for it now? Does the whole of Cork know? Well, they will when I lock this door, ya beautiful empty bastard.

Wasted by Kate Tempest

I'm making a decision.
I'm changing things.
This is it.

Wasted received its world premiere at the Latitude Festival in July 2011, in a joint production between Paines Plough, Birmingham Repertory Theatre and the Roundhouse, and was subsequently revived in 2012 and 2013 as part of two Paines Plough national tours. It was directed by James Grieve.

Context

The first two pages of *Wasted* offer an extended sequence of stage and character descriptions, and include such observations as, 'Sounds of London play out the speakers', Ted is at a 'shitty little desk … Charlotte in the staff room … Danny is sitting on a dingy sofa …'. Three ordinary lives that become, momentarily, like a chorus and admit that they wish they had 'some kind of incredible truth to express', not heroes, but the kind of people who 'feel awkward in theatres'. Kate Tempest's debut play introduces three mid-twenties Londoners – a struggling teacher, a bored office worker, and a musician in a rubbish band. Theatre of the ordinary, theatre of the uneventful twenty-somethings who seem to be waiting, forever waiting, for something but they don't know what. Their lives blur into a sort of tragic hyper-ordinariness through the background noise of drugs, drink and pointless parties. It is only through their combined anonymous voice as 'chorus' that they try to work things out. Tempest's use of language and its near rap-like immediacy is both striking and effective. Will Ted, Charlotte and Danny ever find purpose or direction as easily as they find Ecstasy at a good price?

Acting notes

Mid-twenties Charlotte expresses such a heartbreaking cry of despair. Although she has only recently found herself in the adult world of responsibility and employment, she has the makings of a long and rewarding career as a schoolteacher ahead of her. This is the problem, for she also imagines the horrific prospect of a further forty similar years and this terrifies her to the core. Charlotte is losing what she sees as her definition as a person, and can only see the adult world and the people in it as blurred and smudged images that lack true definition. With her late-teenage years now gone, Charlotte realizes that she actually despises the idea of adult responsibility and sensible behaviour, and yearns for the past. The performance of this speech is dependent on the simple but necessary identification of all the reasons why Charlotte needs to retreat from the adult world. What does her career and newly installed adult life block within her? Notice her frequent use of the personal pronoun 'I' ('I feel like I'm drowning'), in the first section of the speech where she describes her current situation, and then the use of 'we' when she describes the past. Is this a sort of rite-of-passage moment for Charlotte, before she settles down to her career as a schoolteacher or will she reject this for something nearer to what she wants? The difficulty is that in many ways, Charlotte doesn't really know what it is she wants. The speech will not work if it is just played as one long moan about her unfortunate present, but rather, it must explore Charlotte's fears and inability to confront her future.

Charlotte   I'm stood at the front of the class and I feel like I'm
drowning. I'm staring out at them, and I'm thinking who the fuck are
you lot anyway? I look at them, but I can't see children, I can just see
the colour of their jumpers, smudges where their faces should be.

Behind me, today's date is written on the board. I'm trying to pretend I
don't know what it means.

It's hot and the classroom stinks, and the clock's broken and the work
stuck up on the walls is old and the corners are coming away and the
kids are screaming.

I'm trying to remember why I wanted to do this in the first place. You
can't inspire minds on a timetable like this.

I think I'm miserable, Tony.

I mean, I stand in the staffroom in between classes and smile along with
the others, but they're all so bitter, Tony. They're all so fuckin' hateful.
Thirty years in the job, and they hate everything about it, but it's too late
for them to get a new job and I'm pretty sure that secretly they hope the
kids'll come to nothing. I mean it. You should hear the way they talk
about them. No wonder the kids are killing each other over postcodes, or
getting sick at the thought of not being famous.

The classroom's hot, and I'm staring at the kids, and I'm remembering
us lot when we was at school – moving through the corridors like we
was the fuckin' Roman empire. I'm remembering how it felt to be
fifteen, us lot, in a party, feeling like the world was ours, like we fuckin'
owned it. I'm remembering how we cared about each other, how we got
in fights for each other and robbed Tescos and built fires and got off our
faces, it was exciting, wasn't it? It felt real.

What even happened to us? We go parties now, and we've got nothing
to say to each other 'til we're fucked. And even then. We spend hours
talking about parties from before, things that happened to us once, we
spend life retelling life and it's pointless and boring.

The Wolf from the Door by Rory Mullarkey

We don't actually drink coffee
At my coffee morning.
we discuss the violent overthrow of the government. Also there's
flower arranging.

The Wolf From The Door received its world premiere at the Jerwood Theatre Upstairs at the Royal Court Theatre, London, on 10 December 2014. It was directed by James Macdonald.

Context

All order and sanity is lost when a decapitation of a Tesco assistant manager culminates in a series of countrywide uprisings. Rory Mullarkey imagines a sort of breath-taking road trip across middle England where Lady Catherine and her young protégé, Leo, enlist every quaint tearoom, hot yoga class and Women's Institute group on an often violent mission to change the country forever. This is the new post-apocalyptic life after queen Elizabeth II, where revolt begins on station platforms, and the world is a crazy mix of mermaids and skateboards. Oh, and Morris dancers have advanced on Barnet Town Hall waving samurai swords.

Acting notes

Playing a character that is essentially a political idea is difficult in the context of a seemingly comic monologue in that it can become overwhelmed by the logic of the argument and appears more like a manifesto than a living voice or presence. The sheer absurdity of this play – and its most extreme message of revolution and discord – are tough aspects to realize within the space of only a few minutes. 'This was a sign, a message, a signal sent out to revolutionary sleeper agents in hundreds of local community and hobbies groups.' It feels real – but oddly real, something isn't quite right. Caution, therefore; to play a comic or odd revolutionary is to play nobody at all – except cliché. Individuals are not defined by generic labels, but by their action. In the first speech Catherine is angry and feels that she cannot change anything by law. What would drive her to this extreme perspective? Look for the personal clues in the speech; how has she got to this point in her life?

The capital city is all boarded up. The second speech requires the performer to play against any easy sense of apocalyptical archetype – which would be reductive. The extraordinary description of 'sound that tightens somewhere in your body', makes for a vivid performance landscape, in which a direct clear immediate playing style is required. But what drives these words? Is it hate, fear, passion or conviction?

Catherine   This was a sign, a message, a signal sent out to revolutionary sleeper agents in hundreds of local community and hobbies groups across the country to ready the arms they had been stockpiling for the last several months and prepare for assault. At eleven fifteen tomorrow morning those groups will attack the capital and destroy this country's primary political, commercial and social institutions, along with the political, commercial and social elites whose power resides therein. We are not looking forward to this: we are not in love with death and destruction and violence, we are merely tired and sickened by a system which preaches moderation and fairness and equality but in fact merely breeds division and slavery and poverty, in many cases economic, in all cases spiritual. We are sleepwalking through our days. We are not alive, we are merely existing. We are lonely and angry and sad. And this is not only the way this system wants us to be, this is the only way we can be under this system. We cannot change this by law, we cannot change this by raising taxes or voting in people from less privileged backgrounds. If a patient has cancer, do not give them paracetamol: cut off the infested organs and burn them. This is the only way for us to do it. This is the only way to start again.

He was an aristocrat of sorts.

One of the Marquises.

So I'm a 'Lady'

Catherine   It's eleven twenty-three a.m. and we're walking down the
high street
Most of the shops on the high street are closed
We mean closed closed
You know
Boarded up
But there's still the chemist's
You know
Nestled in between the charity shops
And the pawn shops
And the sell-your-gold shops
There's still the chemist's
There's always, always the chemist's
And that's where we're going
You know
It's the chemist's
When we hear this sound rumble in the near middle distance
It sounds like a jangling or tinkling of keys
But of hundreds of keys
On hundreds of key-rings
Somewhere just off in the near middle distance
It's a sound that tightens somewhere in your body
And it's getting louder of course
It's only ever louder
And it's coming from the corner
And as we look on we see cresting the corner
A figure
Two figures
Three figures
More
Then sprinting towards us
A hollering mass
Of white-clothed figures
We duck into the alley
Duck into the side
Between the chemist's and one of the charity shops
And watch as they pass

Making that sound
A sound somehow not like a human sound
But coming from somewhere on human bodies
We glimpse them as they pass
All white
Except their hats
Which
Yellow on their heads
Look made of straw
And as they roar and shout
They swing their axes, chains and huge knives round about
Their heads
And on their legs we see the bells
And one of them
Even though he smudges past, a blur
Is fairly unmistakably
Jeff Thistleton from down the road
Whom we know to be
Extremely active in the local Morris-dancing association
And so we look at each other
You know
Confused

You're Not Like the Other Girls Chrissy by Caroline Horton

At the checkpoint, there are Nazi soldiers with guns. I sit very still.
Monsieur Chevalier rolls down the window and a soldier leans
inside ...

You're Not Like the Other Girls Chrissy was first performed at the
Pleasance Theatre, Edinburgh, on 4 August 2010 by the play's author,
Caroline Horton, produced by China Plate. The piece is about the author's
grandmother. The production was directed by Omar Elerian and Daniel
Goldman.

Context

January 1945, Paris is liberated. Chrissy waits impatiently at the Gare
du Nord for a train to England to be reunited with her English fiancé.
While waiting, she tells stories of her incredible relationship with
her English lover, a teacher who awaits her return. Just before the
outbreak of war, Christiane was sent to Staffordshire to improve her
English and, at Cheadle Tennis Club, Staffordshire, she fell in love
with Cyril. War shattered the possibility of their marriage and kept
them apart for five long years. Sometimes comical, often very moving,
the play's irrepressible spirit was further amplified in the original
production when, at the end of the play, a video was played of the real
Christiane, on her nineteenth birthday, being pushed through Paris in
her wheelchair.

Acting notes

Chrissy is a resilient character who describes her ordeals with brightness
and acceptance. What is remarkable about this testimony is that it is not
a fictionalized account, but the true story and words of a woman in love
at a time of war. The performance challenge would be to identify what is
within her psychological landscape, for she does not openly reveal this.
Chrissy has made very clear choices, to be brave, strong and to get on
with her life, but in so doing, has had to confront the darker more difficult
realities of being alone at war, without the man she loves. Her choice, to
never go to the orchard where people were shot by the Nazis, demonstrates

this selective living and coping strategy. The performance challenge is to demonstrate clearly Chrissy's light, outer or public persona, alongside her inner, darker, survival-thinking mechanism.

Chrissy speaks the English she learnt in North Staffordshire with a strong French accent

Chrissy   In April Cyril came back to Paris with an engagement ring – a pearl. He put it on my finger in the orchard behind our house. It was cherry blossom time. Son of a jeweller and I wait three months for an engagement ring. He also arrive with this enormous pot plant for my mother – a hydrangea – it is horrible and Mamet, she loves it, she calls it Cyril, and she plants it in the front garden. And everybody wants to look at my ring and at the English fiancé ... and I was quite 'the cat with the cream'. And the 'knees of the bees' ... And I can see Cyril and me married ... living in the English countryside. We have a cottage with our own cherry blossom tree. And we ride our bicycles and walk our golden retriever and own a Rolls Royce with an English number plate.

15th April 1939, we said goodbye on platform fourteen. Over there. Six years ago. He left and the war arrive.

I never go to our orchard now. During the occupation people were taken there by the Nazis and shot.

(*Sits on cases to talk to us gently.*) In the beginning, it was such a funny war, nothing happened. Cyril and me write each other every week and I took a job as governess for little Annique in Fontainebleu. I live with her and her grandmother, who we call *la Gouvernement* and her nose would drip into her teacup plop plop.

Geoffrey Colman is Head of Acting at the Royal Central School of Speech and Drama. As an acting coach, he has collaborated with many national and international theatre, film and TV practitioners, and has a longstanding association with the Theatre Royal Haymarket as a 'resident master'. Recent award-winning theatre credits include *I Loved You and I Loved You* (Sweetshop Revolution / National Theatre Wales), *Justitia* (Jasmin Vardimon Company / Peacock Theatre, London), *PARK* (Jasmin Vardimon Company / Sadlers Wells, London). TV/film coaching credits include *Britain's Next Top Model* (Sky Living), *Mother of Invention* (HBO/Sky 1), extensive work with BAFTA award-winning mentalist & hypnotist, Derren Brown, including *Miracles For Sale* (Channel 4), *Fear & Faith/Placebo* (Channel 4), *Apocalypse* (Channel 4), *The Push*, (Channel 4 / Vaudeville Productions), and also with mentalist and illusionist Katherine Mills *Mind Games* (Watch TV). Film coaching includes *Kick Ass 2* (Marv Films/Universal Pictures, directed by Jeff Wadlow). Geoffrey Colman writes for The Stage and lectures on a wide range of performance-related issues (National Portrait Gallery, National Theatre, ICA, etc.). He also regularly broadcasts on BBC (Radio 3/Free Thinking, Radio 4/The Why Factor, and BBC World Service/Weekend etc.). Bloomsbury Methuen Drama recently published his introduction to Steven Berkoff's *One Act Plays*.